Children of Character I

Bill and Mardy Freeman

Mardy Freeman
Bill

Freeman Family Publishers
25467 SW First Avenue
Newberry, FL 32669
www.thefreemans.org

Children of Character I
Published by Freeman Family Publishers

© 2001 by Bill and Mardy Freeman

All Scripture references are either direct quotations or
paraphrased from the King James Bible.

Cover art by Patrick Freeman

ISBN: 9 780972 492676

Freeman Family Publishing
25467 SW First Avenue
Newberry, FL 32669
www.thefreemans.org

Third Edition: April 2007

Children of Character I

To our children, Jonathan, James, Kathryn, Daniel, Stephen, Patrick, and Joel ~

We have no greater joy than to know that our children are walking in truth. III John 1:4

Table of Contents

Curriculum Blues

By Mardy Freeman

I had found the curriculum that we should be using.
It was fun. It was bright. And it wasn't confusing.
But just as I started to write out the check
I discovered a new one was much better yet.

I had written *that* check when I suddenly read
That *another* new program was better instead.
So I dutifully researched and found it was true.
This one *was* better – yes, all the way through!

"This one looks perfect!" I said to myself.
"Not a piece of this resource will sit on the shelf."
It was simple, yet timeless. Its methods were flawless.
With only one glitch – it cost nine thousand dollars.

I had thirty-nine dollars and fifty-three cents,
So off for curriculum fliers I sent.
And they came on one day – all four hundred five.
I answered the door and was buried alive!

My children revived me and gave me a kiss
And it suddenly dawned on me what I had missed!
It matters less *what they know* than it does *who they are!*
With strong moral character, my kids will go far!

Determination and courage are worth much more than talents.
So teaching them *character* will keep them in balance.
Then encouraging them to reason, to ask and to think,
To wade through the waters of knowledge and drink.

Education's not just what I pull from the shelf;
It's in giving my children a part of myself!
I see now they'll learn it – one way or the other.
But, lately my kids are in need of their mother!

The fliers I saved for a few weeks from now
When I know I'll be desperately wondering how
To implement all of my newfound ideals
And scrambling again for incredible deals.

In the meantime, should you find the one that beats all
And stumble across it some time before fall,
If it teaches *me* how to do all these things –
Please pick up the phone and give me a ring!

You may be thinking to yourself, "I don't homeschool and I never will. This book is not for me." We encourage you to read it anyway. It's really a book about developing character in your children. Our family just learned most of our lessons during the course of homeschooling. Having our children with us through school, ministry, work and fun simply compressed the time it took to learn these lessons. What we share will still be applicable to you and your family regardless of how your children are being educated. Our purpose is to share the lessons we learned in that lifestyle, not (necessarily) the lifestyle itself.

Whenever we speak we get the question, "My children are (fill-in-the-blank) years old. Which book would be best for me?" We usually say that *Children of Character I* is a great place to start, especially if you see issues being exposed in your own heart through your children. If you're looking for practical help on sheltering young children and preparing teens for adulthood *Children of Character II* would be a good choice.

Introduction

I walked into the end of the year homeschool program with a sense of finality and relief, having just completed my first – and what I was sure would be my last – year of homeschooling. My husband wanted us to continue, but I felt under-qualified to take the place of a college-trained teacher in my child's life. And with a six year-old, a toddler and a new baby, I was feeling the need for a break. I also wanted more time to spend with the younger ones, as well as to reclaim some personal time.

The program that night had no videos about homeschooling, no special speakers and no workshops. So, no one was more surprised than I, when two hours later, I walked out of that event totally dedicated to homeschooling!

What did I see that night that so thoroughly changed my mind? It was the children. There was a depth of character in the older home educated children that I hadn't seen in any group of young people that we'd previously known or worked with. It was the type of character I wanted to see develop in my own children. While other parents watched performances and promotions, I watched preteen boys and girls respectfully give their attention to the program. I later listened as they talked to each other about their studies, their activities, their thoughts and their worlds – without artificial masks or foolishness or pretentiousness. There were no cliques or out-of-place clothing or "statements" being made. Yet, there was no legalistic atmosphere, nor any sense of fear in the children (or in the parents) that someone would break a rule or misbehave. They were at ease with their parents, respectful to their parents' friends, polite to strangers, and the most impressive to me – they were inclusive of their siblings. They seemed genuinely comfortable with themselves, with each other and with the world. It was an event I would later rank as a 90 to 95 on an imaginary "Character Scale."

Until then I had only seen the potential cost of homeschooling, but that night I saw the potential product. I was so impressed that I came into instant agreement with Bill, and found myself signing a blank contract with God that said, "If homeschooling is what I have to do to get that type of character, then to homeschooling I'm committed!"

Little did I know then that a year after that inspiring decision I would make my first truly ground-breaking revelation about the relationship between homeschooling and developing character: *Having my kids spend all day with me was not going to produce strong character!* As a matter of fact, instead of *developing* character, it seemed my children were only *becoming* characters!

That humbling realization propelled us onto an exciting, difficult, rewarding, terrifying, wonderful journey with our children that has had more surprise mountains, valleys and turns than we could have ever imagined.

We hope each one who reads this book will be encouraged as you seek to build character in your children. Please don't compare yourself or your children to us, or to anyone else. We have learned mostly in tiny baby steps (sometimes one forward, then several backward until we stumble), and it's taken many years of trials and errors, tears and sorrows, mistakes and failures. Many other families are much "farther along" than we are. We try to not compare their successes with our failures. None of us are more important than another; only the truths we've learned are important. When we cry out to the Lord for help and apply the truths He reveals, we reap good fruit; when we forget or revert back to our old ways, we see the same type of conflicts and struggles as before. Let us each compare our selves only to Christ – and cry out to God for His mercy and grace for help in time of need.

Call to Me, and I will answer you, and show you great and wonderful things which you do not know. Jeremiah 33:33

Chapter One: Decide on Character!

*My son, 1) give me your heart and
2) let your eyes observe my ways.*
Proverbs 23:26

"**W**ILL YOU PLEASE BE PATIENT?!" I, er, *remarked emphatically* to our seven-year old as I covered the receiver. He had just interrupted me for the third time and I didn't want to explain to him again that he shouldn't interrupt me on the phone unless it was urgent. Settling another dispute between him and his younger brother would just have to wait until I was finished. Besides, I was placing a long-distance call at Bill's request, getting information for a seminar where we could learn more about teaching character to our children. If my child didn't realize how important that was, couldn't he at least remember that one simple rule?

I'd no sooner hung up the phone before I was summoned to the boys' room by the argument. I marched down the hall in determined-mommy fashion to get to the bottom of it. But, as I rounded the corner into their room, I heard something that made me stop in my tracks.

"WILL YOU PLEASE BE PATIENT?!" our son had just, er, *yelled impatiently* at his little brother. I gulped hard as I listened to my own words being shouted in the very same tone that I'd used only a few minutes before. I suddenly had the feeling that perhaps I wouldn't need a special seminar to diagnose at least one of the problems we were facing.

Why it hit me so clearly that particular day, I don't know. Nevertheless, I saw a tangible, real-life connection between my son's behavior and mine. I experienced the painful realization that children do, indeed, learn what they live.[1]

Translated, that meant that with all the best character seminars and curriculum in the world, I could not yell, *"WILL YOU PLEASE BE PATIENT!?"* one moment, and successfully teach the character quality of patience the next.

Lest you think this revelation too basic, let me say that I've spent most of my prime years since that day making other lab-tested discoveries, such as:

- We can't teach children contentment – if we complain when the car breaks down or that the vacation must be canceled.
- It's nearly impossible to instill respect for authority – if we break traffic laws to get them to the band concert on time.
- We can't expect children to learn forgiveness – if we hold grudges against others.

To decide that character will be first in our child's life is to decide that it will be first in our own. We're always training our children in character whether we realize it or not because we reveal our own character to those with whom we live, and children learn by example.

We're always training our children in character whether we realize it or not because we reveal our own character to those with whom we live, and children learn by example.

Of course, our children have their own sin natures, and their very own sets of weaknesses and flaws which are often different from our own. But, these tend to be a little easier for us to help them with because we can teach by example as well as by instruction.

Character truly is more caught than taught. And daily interaction is the most powerful character-training lesson of all, much more effective than any planned teaching on character qualities. That was the hard lesson that forced me to realize that home education alone would not produce the character for which I was hoping. The painful truth was that I was going to have to look more closely at myself if I wanted to teach character to my children.

Academics

Deciding our children's character is most important doesn't mean they sacrifice academic excellence, or that we substitute character for academics. Quite the contrary. It means our children are more likely to do better academically, athletically, musically, or in any area if their character development is strengthened. Character doesn't replace quality in our children's accomplishments; it enhances it – for all the right reasons. It should be the foundation on which we lay further instruction.

How tempting it's been for me, though, to settle for academic mastery or a winning performance as the goal, but miss more foundational issues such as humility, loyalty, dependability, responsibility or faith. Strong character is the soil from which excellence rises. Too often in our hurried lifestyles and performance-centered culture we minimize its significance.

Our children's "best," however, may not be a sibling's best, the club's best, the test's best or the state's best. Deciding on character means that we teach our children to do their best because it's right, because it pleases God and because it's good for them. It means that we don't place undue weight on the product (the competition, the performance, the project, the piece), or encourage a child to do his best because he'll receive our approval, grandparent approval, the grand prize, the scholarship, the trophy, or eventually the right job or connections. That would be training our children to be performance-centered, approval-centered or goal-centered, a pattern that will lead to being project-centered, career-centered, money-centered or power-centered. That doesn't mean our children never compete with others, but that they understand that they are ultimately competing only with themselves. A competitive center can also develop imbalanced priorities.

Testing

Our state, Florida, allows standardized nationally-normed testing as an option for annual reporting. Some states require it. Because our state doesn't require testing, we postpone formal testing until the middle school years. Our children simply enjoy what they're learning more when they know they don't have to study for a test on it. We have the freedom to take a detour from the text to focus more on a particular topic that interests them. We also discovered that holding formal testing off until middle school years has been enough time to prepare our children to nab scholarships and do well in college-level studies.

There is an incredible internal pressure on most new homeschool parents, especially on us moms, to "produce" an academic product better than the local schools. After all we've said, in effect, to the state, "I can do a better of job teaching my child than you can." And testing, we know, is grading the teacher as well as the student!

But many parents have no degree in education. Even parents with education degrees can feel intimidated by the task of taking their own child's education into their hands. It can be even more intimidating for us if we require them to submit to annual standardized testing if they're not required to by the state. It can also be intimidating to children in the elementary years.

How tempting it is for parents to be anxious over test results. Worry can set in just before testing day arrives.

What if my child understands the concepts, but doesn't perform well? What if he doesn't even understand the concepts? What if he's not at his grade level yet? What if he's not a good test-taker? What will the results say about my child? What will they say about me?

If our children succeed in testing, but fail in the little things, where character development begins, they won't reach their potential.

And what if our children do well – or extremely well? Are we overly pleased? How much of a relief is that knowledge? How much value do we place on that score? How does that knowledge affect our children's attitudes – about themselves or about others?

Our children need to understand that high scores and good test results aren't goals; they're merely things that usually begin to happen when someone masters the material. They also need to understand that there are those who do understand the concepts, but aren't good test-takers. If our children succeed in testing, but fail in the little things, where character development begins, they won't reach their potential.

Of course, we don't think it's wrong for parents to use standardized testing in the elementary years. But annual standardized testing for younger students can set children and parents up for comparison, pride and fear, and often produces a higher stress level. Instead of showing how much material a student has mastered, standardized tests score how well the test-taker scored compared with everyone else. If a student becomes stressed or discouraged if he scores poorly or stumbles with pride if he excels, or if we see we're putting too much emphasis on the results, standardized testing should be bypassed.

We use standardized testing to prepare our children for entrance requirements into college. We begin testing (using test-prep materials for the PSAT,[2] SAT,[3] ACT,[4] CPT,[5] CLEPS or other tests that relate to their individual goals) at the beginning of high school when there's still plenty of time for preparation, and when academic achievement typically comes easier.

If our child's testing causes undue worry (or excessive satisfaction), or if it causes us to take character shortcuts as we prepare them for testing, or to adopt an end-justifies-the-means mentality, then character is slipping from being the most important issue. In addition, if a family is enrolled in a more formal educational program, even where the parent does a portion of the teaching, it will be challenging to find time for working on issues of the heart when needed if there are numerous academic or testing requirements throughout the year.

Teaching character is not "unschooling," where the *child* determines the course or rate of education. Nor is it rigidly following a curriculum – where a *textbook* determines the course or rate of our child's education. Teaching character means that *parents* determine the course and rate of education, beginning with character needs of the child.

The ideal situation is to have the freedom to break from academics from time to time when it's needed to till the soil of a child's heart, to try to keep it soft (teachable and humble) and rich (strong in character). Then we can toss academic seeds onto that good soil and they'll have a better chance of growing healthy and strong. Our children will have a better motivation for learning. This is teaching the whole person and can help them reach their potential.

Evaluations

Another way our state allows for compliance to the home education law is through a year-end evaluation by a certified teacher. We prefer evaluations with a teacher over standardized testing for many reasons. The most important reason is that standardized testing is designed to compare what is in the *mind* with other *minds*. Year-end evaluations can help a parent evaluate a child on many levels, including character development.

We have been so helped and encouraged by annual evaluations with a Christian home-education-friendly teacher that we suggest to parents whose states don't require them to consider evaluations for the many benefits.

During an evaluation academics can be assessed in a less formal setting with an evaluator rather than an unfamiliar testing site. Public and private-schooled children are already familiar with their surroundings for testing, but a home educated child must take in a new environment and new faces on test day.

Secondly, a certified teacher-evaluator can provide necessary sample testing on a much smaller scale, which can give the same overall picture as a day of standardized testing.

In addition, the whole person, not just the mind, can be evaluated, "Laura's reading comprehension has come up two grade levels this year." An evaluator can also give a more personalized assessment not found on a standardized test, "However, her handwriting could use improvement." An evaluator can offer experienced advice, "Have you tried any math manipulatives to help Kyle with these concepts?" An evaluator can also be a source of support and encouragement in character, "Suzie, how neat your math papers are! Your improved scores are clearly a result of your attention to accuracy and detail this year!" An evaluator can even write an evaluation based on teaching the whole child, which can include character development alongside academic performance if we request it. Evaluators can check not only academic progress, but point out weak spots in our teaching or methods, suggest proven alternatives, hold our hand when we need encouragement and also commend our children for character development. Therefore, a family that wants to focus on character may want to consider year-end evaluations over standardized testing (or alongside it if it's required) until high school. Even if year-end evaluations are not required, they are a great tool.

But character has to become more important than year-end evaluations, too. When one of our sons was about ten, we decided it was time to try to get to the root of some of his resistance and willfulness. In my naïveté and performance-oriented fashion, I think I may have scheduled one evening for this project. I can't remember now – I may have scheduled even less time than that! But, it took months of listening, sharing, praying, trying to understand, forgiving, asking for forgiveness, patiently listening again, patiently forgiving again, more sharing and more praying. I had to keep at it, being willing to put the schedule down to listen to issues of the heart over and over before we saw changes in attitude that lasted.

Changing character *became* the class. I had to be willing to stop and listen, knowing I might have to say to our evaluator that we only finished half the math book or a portion of our other texts during the year. That was very hard for me to do! Many times I was guilty of not addressing the character needs of my children because I was afraid they'd get behind academically, or not have enough paperwork or academic mastery to make an acceptable evaluation. I worried that if I invested twenty minutes during the school day listening to a child explain what was really bothering him (he was mad at his brother), and then tried to gently teach him how to forgive him (which was why he was tossing dead flies at him instead of finishing his math), then he might not finish his math lesson that day. If I then took more time to help his brother understand the importance of being a good steward of another's property (because he had angered him by leaving his glow-in-the-dark snake where the dog could chew it up), then he, too, might get behind in reading or grammar. And if I brought *his* academics to a halt, making sure he cleaned up *all* of the glow-in-the-dark dog throw-up from every single tassel on the Oriental rug before it dried (so that he learned consequences for his behavior and how to be faithful in little things), and he then became even further behind – and if we lived like that day after day –what would I tell our evaluator? How would I feel if their friends (or siblings) passed them academically? How would they feel?

When I analyzed my own motives I saw that many times I was more concerned with their academic standing or my fear of a weak evaluation than with their character development. What I had failed to realize during those early years was that we wouldn't be working on the same character issues for the rest of their lives – even though, at times, it truly felt like we would.

Today, over twenty years later, I can tell you that our children's education was not being *derailed* by character issues; it was being *established* by them.   At this printing, we've graduated four students and are still home educating three.   The graduates are each doing what they believe God has called them to do, and are stronger in character today than they would have been had I forced them to stay on the academic wagon when I saw we needed to make a character pit-stop. I'm so grateful to the Lord for the times I did stop to check my own heart and then listen to theirs. I regret those times I pushed them on, telling myself I didn't have time to take hearts and life-issues into consideration. I sometimes wonder about how much better our children might have done had I yielded to conviction a little better, softened my approach a little sooner. But, the Lord knows that we moms wonder about things like that, doesn't He?   And He comforts us with forgiveness for yesterday, comfort for today and hope for tomorrow.

> Impressive bookwork is a poor substitute for character, and excellence within does begin to produce excellence without.

Documenting Character

Stopping to tenderly work with heart attitudes and character issues can bring major changes in the school day that interrupt academics. That can feel a little unnerving if we view our work with our children's hearts as an interruption to school, especially when an evaluation is looming in front of us.

There were many interruptions to academics that first year. Rather than saying, "Stop arguing and get your math done," I began to stop what I was doing and listen to what was really bothering a child. That found me spending hours listening, talking, praying, working on my own perspective and attitudes (because many times I really didn't want to stop what I was doing), counseling, sharing, trying to understand, working on my own perspective and attitudes (because I didn't seem to be able to see much improvement in the situation after so much investment), reviewing the same lessons, counseling again and working on my own perspective and attitudes *again* (because I'd begun to allow fear to drive me *again* rather than letting the Holy Spirit lead me).

Even though I'd spent months working with my children on life lessons, I didn't think to document a single hour of the time. I had the wrong mind-set that it couldn't be considered "school" if it didn't fit into the standard academic mold. Consequently, along with fewer workbooks, which were *not* filled to overflowing with neat, right answers, and skinnier folders *not* filled with star-laden paperwork, I also had little proof that we were indeed teaching our children – though it seemed it was all I ever did.

> Teaching children how to forgive and be forgiven, how to get to root problems, how to accept being under authority and how to grasp truths about self-acceptance are important life-skills.

I didn't realize that teaching our children how to forgive and be forgiven, how to get to root problems, how to accept being under authority, how to grasp truths about self-acceptance and how to receive instruction on the ways of life concerning personal development, interpersonal relationships and conflict resolution were all very important life-skills. The next year I began documenting my time and the topics we discussed. Our year-end evaluation became much less stressful for me.

Teaching character is not the same as not teaching anything

and calling it character training. It's actual documentable training for real life for which we want to prepare our children. That preparation can, and should, be documented – even if we just label it as an ongoing course in Life-Skills. What we call it is not that important. But, if we're teaching the whole person, and not just the mind, it's a good idea to record it.

Impressive bookwork is a poor substitute for character, and excellence within does begin to produce excellence without.

Evaluators[6]

If we decide to focus on character, it's important to choose an evaluator who shares your vision for character training. Most areas have lists of certified evaluators available, and there are plenty of evaluators who understand the importance of character training.

It's important to explain your goals before hiring an evaluator to see if they're on the same page, or if, instead, they have concerns we don't share. When you find a good evaluator, it's important to stay with them from one year to the next, working on any areas that may have been a concern to them the year before. It's easier for an evaluator to help you with a true assessment if he or she can work with the same student every year.

If character training begins to take up more time than expected, as ours did, it's a good idea to check in with your evaluator during the year to make sure there are no major concerns. We didn't do that the first year and surprised our evaluator with less visible work than what was expected. Of course, I had no idea at the beginning of that year that we wouldn't accomplish all of our character goals within the first few weeks! Little or no communication puts undue pressure on an evaluator and can bring an unfavorable evaluation. We later called our evaluator for mid-year advice when one of our children, whose character growth was strong, continued to stall academically. It gave me a some relief to know that she not only would be expecting to see less academic progress from that child, but that *she* had been the one to suggest that we slow his academic pace for the year.

An evaluator who shares our goals and holds our hand can be a strong encouragement to stay on the character track during times of pressure.

Well-meaning Advice

Parents should be used to getting advice! Additionally, when parents in any generation do something other than what the culture expects it usually brings even more advice.

> We can't expect our children to honor us and forgive us when we give bad advice - which every parent does from time to time - if we don't honor and forgive our own parents when they give bad advice.

When we receive advice about the educational choices we're making for our children, we do have the right (and duty) to humbly judge the fruit of the advice-giver. We can ask ourselves, "Do they or their children have the type of character we want to see developing in our children?"

If the answer is yes, it would be wise to listen to their advice with an open heart and mind, even though the exact path their family chose may be different than the one ours is supposed to choose.

If the answer is no, it doesn't automatically mean the advice isn't worthy. Their children may be resistant or perhaps the advice-givers don't apply their advice in their own lives. Perhaps their children haven't been exposed to their good advice long enough to show progress. Bad fruit is definitely cause to examine the advice more carefully, but not cause to completely reject it. Sometimes people who aren't walking in a truth can still speak truth to us. We need to be able to judge the advice as with or without merit, but without judging the advisor. That can take a lot of humility, vulnerability – and grace.

Sometimes well-meaning advice comes from parents, grandparents or other relatives. We do want to honor our parents.[7] The word "honor" means to give great weight to their words. But we have to determine if their advice is contrary to advice or commands in Scripture. We're not supposed to give so much weight to parental counsel that it keeps us from fulfilling our God-given duty to bring our children up in the nurture and admonition of the Lord. Jesus said it would be better if a millstone were hung about our necks and we were cast into the sea than for us to "cause one of these little ones to stumble."[8] A millstone of God's judgment is a much greater weight than the weight of parental counsel. Obedience to parents cannot trump obedience to God. Jesus Himself tells us to love God more than father or mother.[9]

On the other hand, relatives, especially parents, can sometimes see our faults quite clearly and may want to help us with them – especially if they think those faults are going to affect their grandchildren. If there are any unresolved issues between parents and grown children, it will be tempting to automatically reject their advice, no matter how much truth may be in it.

A good indicator of whether other issues are clouding our ability to hear advice clearly is our own reaction factor. Does other people's concern irritate us? Does their advice get under our skin? Do we use the energy in those negative feelings to keep us going our own way? Does fear of displeasing them paralyze us? These issues will carry over into the next generation affecting our character and our children's character unless we acknowledge them, and ask the Lord to set us free from them.

The "Lord's Prayer" reminds us that we need to forgive (release completely) everyone in order to be forgiven by our Heavenly Father (forgive us, as we forgive those who sin against us).[10] If we're receiving unsolicited or flawed advice from others, and it seems especially irritating, we need to ask God for the grace to forgive them, the strength to honor them, and wisdom to make the right decision.[11] We can't expect our children to honor us and forgive us when we give bad advice - which every parent does from time to time - if we don't honor and forgive our own parents when they give bad advice.

Extra-Curricular Activities

There are numerous extra-curricular activities available for children today from academic clubs and competitions to sporting events and the arts. The home education student is no exception. In many states local schools offer part-time enrollment, dual-enrollment and online enrollment. A home educated student can often participate in band, play on the football team, take foreign language, science or computer classes while also competing in academic or community events.

Is there anything wrong with those activities? Of course not. Not in and of themselves. There's always something good that can be learned in an outside-the-home activity – whether it's becoming a better speller by competing in the spelling bee, learning team spirit by playing on the basketball team or gaining musical skills by taking lessons.

Choosing character, however, means that we don't automatically follow the crowd into all those activities, but we make decisions based on what's best for our child. If our child does participate in competitions or activities, it means we don't let him cut ethical corners when he's under a time deadline, even though no one else will know. It means we allow him to lose the competition when he doesn't get the project finished on time. It means we choose to refrain from helping (or nagging) so much that the emphasis becomes the project and not the lessons learned from completing the project. And if we see that his skills in any area are outstanding, but attitudes of pride or conceit or self-importance are beginning to creep in, it means we're willing to hold him back in that skill until his character is better developed.

> Our motivations are what we'll pass on to the next generation, whether we plan to or not.

To decide on character means that character takes precedence over what everyone else is doing. It means we know why we do what we do, and why our child is involved, or not involved, in activities or programs outside the home. It means that we have to take some time and effort, even when it seems we can't afford it, to look deeply into our own motivations. Those motivations are what we'll pass on to the next generation, whether we plan to or not.

The "Baaah" Factor

When our children were younger we felt we needed to pull them out of extra-curricular activities. We had to walk alone, so to speak, apart from what most of our friends were doing with their children. A successful parent usually has to do a certain amount of walking alone somewhere along the line, sometimes going against the flow in extended families, our own social group or even within a local church. It can feel tempting to follow, for once, wherever others are going, doing whatever others are doing – because it's where someone else *is* going and is what someone else *is* doing.

We call this strong pull to do what others are doing the "Baaah factor." Who wants to walk alone? Not me! It feels more secure to hang out and bleat contentedly with the rest of the sheep. But, the Shepherd loves to call His sheep apart to quiet, lonely paths, even away from other sheep from time to time so we can learn to hear and follow His voice above all others.[12]

It was hard for me to think about pulling our children out of their fun activities to focus more on character. Were we sure we were supposed to pull them out? No one else seemed to be pulling their children out. What if we were overreacting to small character flaws that would eventually go away on their own? I worried that our children might be upset by our decision. What if they didn't understand why we were removing them? How strange we looked and how lonely I felt.

Like sheep, I enjoyed the security of the other sheep very much. There were times I wanted that security even more than a closer (less secure-feeling) walk of obedience with the Shepherd. If we sense a lot of pressure when we think about being different from other "sheep," we're probably deriving our security from the wrong place.

To achieve great things for God, and training the next generation in strong character is right near the top of that list, we need to be attentive and obedient to the Shepherd's voice.

Sometimes His voice will lead us to participate in something, sometimes to decline. When we can tell the difference and make our decisions based on obedience to His will for our own family, then we can help our children learn how to be attentive and obedient to His voice for their own lives. We need to be willing to do what we believe is right for our own children, even when no one else understands, agrees or goes with us. Our children are worth it, and their character is worth it.

Our Friends and Their Peers

Character must also become more important than the successes of others. When our niece or nephew, or our friends' children win the spelling bee or the scholarship, or earn their A.A. while still in high school, we might feel pressure to speed up the academics. Our children might feel more pressure to compete or perform.

While there's nothing wrong with spelling bees, scholarships or AA's in high school, if we allow our children to slide in areas of character so they can produce a higher academic standing, we've placed performance over character. This is especially hard when we've just begun to focus on character, but we aren't sure we see any results yet. We can get the feeling that our children will miss out on something important, or that we may not know what we're doing after all. Even if we realize that our child's need to discover heroes of courage and faith is greater than his need to excel in another skill, it takes a strong commitment to his character to keep him on the right path.

Math is the hardest subject to catch up, so we did try to make sure at least some math was done each day. But, it's amazing how easily most other academics can be caught up in the middle or high school years. One day when Jon was about fifteen he walked in while I was going over a grammar lesson with one of his brothers and said, "Hey, Mom. What's a verb again?" I can't describe the panic and feelings of self-doubt and failure that enveloped me with that simple question. *How could he possibly be fifteen and not know what a verb is? Did we never finish grammar? What kind of a mother am I? What kind of a future will he have?*

I apologized to Jon, handed him the fifth and sixth grade grammar books, and asked him to study them. A sense of mommy-guilt and self-questioning plagued me for the remainder of the year, and I began to wonder about the importance of character when my son would have to sit for an SAT or CPT, earn a degree, or one day earn enough money to support a family.

Jon, however, had been growing in character - along with me – for five years. So, when I handed him the grammar books he chewed them up and ate them like candy. He then consumed the next one, and the next. That was 1996. One year later at the age of sixteen he passed CLEP[13] exams earning eighteen college credits in one sitting, and a year after that snagged a four-year college scholarship with his SAT scores. He went on to graduate cum laude from the University of Florida, as well as cum laude from the Oak Brook College of law, and is now happily married and practicing law with his law school sweetheart. Jon made significant improvement in his character development first, and still had time in his high school years to fill in some academic "holes."

On the other hand, our second child, James, was a classic right-brain dominant male (more on that in Chapter Four) who loved music and absolutely excelled in hands-on projects. James' character was strong and he had very good judgment and common sense. But he had very little love for academics other than reading classics and listening to good music. Because we decided James' character would remain foremost, he was allowed to progress academically commensurate with his ability, rather than be pushed to keep up with state or national standards. Consequently, he developed an incredibly healthy self-esteem and confidence about his place in the world. He knew he was supposed to bypass college to fulfill his dream of becoming a landlord.[14] James is now an adult and well on his way to fulfilling that dream.

If we focus on our children's character, they can blossom according to their own timetable and in their own unique way, which can help them find their path in life a little more easily.

Big Heads/Small Hearts

It's always better for a child's character to be growing at a faster rate than his other talents whether academic, sports, musical, the arts or otherwise. When a child excels in any area other than character first, he can be tempted to believe he's more deserving than others who are less accomplished than himself. He can grow a big head (he knows a lot or can do a lot) and a small heart (he focuses primarily on himself, with little or no concern for the needs of those around him).

To be smart is to know the right answer; to be wise is to know when to speak and when to remain silent. To be smart is to score high marks and perhaps receive admiration and awards; to be wise is to do one's best even when it's not possible to win. Smartness *is* an asset, but without wisdom it erodes into a liability. We've all known people who were smart, perhaps brilliant, but whose brilliance we could have lived without. We have too many examples today of what kind of leadership knowledge without character produces.

It can be hard for us to recognize pride in our own children, and usually impossible for a child to discern it in himself without help. Pride can be very subtle, but it's very serious because God says that He resists the proud.[15] If parents have a lot of pride, it's easier for children to pick it up, and they, too, suffer the consequences. Pride also keeps us blind to our own faults, to our children's faults, to others' needs and to God's blessings.

I think of home educated children as flowers being raised in a greenhouse rather than in a big garden or in the wild. Greenhouse flowers bloom more (and more rapidly) than those on the outside, not because they are inherently different than other flowers, but because they respond to their environment. We want our children to understand that their talents, as well as their environment, are gifts. When they understand that they'll have the joy of discovering the purpose for which they were given those talents. We also need to understand that we're simply stewards of the Master's greenhouse, and make sure we're encouraging good character to bloom, rather than just talents.

> We have too many examples today of what kind of leadership knowledge without character produces.

Burn-Out

Besides developing big heads and small hearts, children who are pushed to excel tend to either burn out and rebel, or grow up performance-oriented and driven.[16] In addition, children who excel beyond their years, whether they're pushed or are pushing themselves, trade in many hours (and sometimes years) of their childhood.

Replacing Activities with Ministry

If we look at extra-curricular activities as diversions until our children "get through a phase," we run the risk of burying real problems, postponing the inevitable. Unresolved problems usually don't go away on their own, but resurface later when they're harder to fix. Our children were taking top honors in extra-curricular activities in their elementary and middle-school years when we decided to pull them out. How right it was for us to pull them away from activities where they excelled because their character wasn't yet strong.

We started replacing our old activities with ministry opportunities such as taking food to needy seniors and visiting nursing homes. It took a while, but what a difference we began to see in our children (and in us). Our focus, and later our children's focus, began to shift from, "What will we get/learn/earn from this activity?" to, "What can we give to this person?" or, "How can we be a part of the solution?" Our whole family became a little less whiny, a little less complacent and a little more proactive. We even began to see people's lives change even if in very small ways because of something we did. That was inspirational.

Instead of competing against others mentally or physically or musically (though we don't think competition is wrong), our children began working as a team alongside friends – old and new – to accomplish a common good. It was a great feeling since true teamwork, purely for someone else's good, forms great bonds of fellowship. It was one of those life-calibrating decisions we've never regretted.

Conclusion

Strong character is the foundation on which we want to build academic excellence because it will save our children (and us) from a myriad of troubles including pride, foolishness and vanity. If we teach them that it's better to be wise first and then smart, they'll be able to more easily handle their own successes. Character reminds them that true learning isn't just what they know – it's what they *do* with what they know.

To decide on character means that we compare ourselves (and our children) not to others, but to God's standards, where sins, weaknesses and failures point out our need of a Savior, and strengths and talents are recognized as gifts. It means that our children's character has to be more important to us than test results (even end-of-the-year testing), annual evaluations, grandparent understanding, our best friend's approval or a club's activities or events. Their character development needs to be more important than competitions or scholarships, or once-in-a-lifetime opportunities that tempt us (or them) to cut corners or to temporarily embrace an end-justifies-the-means mentality.

It's not possible to predict what our children will be when they grow up. But if we can help them to grow up with strong character, they will most likely be the best they can be in whatever they do. What they *do* will not matter as much as who they *are*. And who they are will help guide them to make the best choices in what they do.

I scheduled that character-training seminar that day that our child interrupted me on the phone. There were things in it that helped us and things we later had to discard. But the revelation that came to me standing outside our son's door – that children really do learn what they live – has been my most valuable lesson. It forced me to look at my own character first that day. It's the reality that helps keep me in check today.

If we commit to making character first and foremost, it will play out hundreds of ways over hundreds of days as we relate to our children, and nip untold problems in the bud. If we decide that the effort will be too great, we do them, the church and society a disservice. Character has to become more important than anything else.

Chapter Two: Begin with the Heart

If I take care of my character, my reputation will take care of itself. Dwight L. Moody

The heart is the place where character is developed. To decide that character will be foremost in our children's education is to commit to beginning with the heart.

The difficulty in this is that we parents have to be willing to let our own hearts be changed if we hope to be instruments of change in our children's heart. Lasting positive influence rarely takes place, especially in the areas of values and faith, where hypocrisy exits or where there is little or no respect. I know because I tried to teach my children to adopt values and faith that I wasn't living up to myself. It just doesn't work. Even today, if I see myself start slipping back into my old hypocritical parenting style with almost-grown children *(Do what I say, not what I do),* I begin to see tiny sprouts of the same old weeds that used to overtake good fruit.

> Lasting positive influence rarely takes place, especially in the areas of values and faith, where hypocrisy exits or where there is little or no respect.

All learning becomes more meaningful, more purposeful, and more real if the teacher is also teachable, and the heart is considered. We have to go back to square one and begin with the heart – first ours, and then theirs.

Winning Their Hearts vs. Winning Their Favor

Winning a child's heart is keeping a oneness of fellowship and understanding between us without compromising God's standards.

Our words and actions as well as our attitudes, motivations and reactions make it either easy or hard for our children to trust us with their hearts. Parenting allows a unique and wonderful position to work with our children's hearts.

We don't want to confuse winning their hearts with winning their favor. If we think we have to win their favor, we'll eventually lose their respect – and their hearts as well.

I'll never forget a side trip I once took with friends to a planned "perfect community." As we drove past picture-perfect families walking down picture-perfect streets, I couldn't help feeling a bit saddened for the picture-perfect children in those affluent, picture-perfect houses who were being showered with more material goods than they needed. How hard it is to forge strong character when one's environment is so pleasant and one's life so easy. Jesus said it would be hard for a rich man to enter the Kingdom of Heaven.[17]

When we don't know what to do…

Accept the Problem.

Ask.

Listen.

Obey.

Most of us parents sincerely want what's *best* for our children. But, parents who give the best *things* to their children, including the best academic or extra-curricular opportunities, can rob them of some of life's best lessons. There are some things that must be earned, or experienced at an older age to be truly appreciated.

A warm and loving home with firm boundaries, and parents who display faith in God and mutual respect for one another constitute the ideal living and learning environment for any child. This ideal seemed achievable to me when we planned our family, but I quickly faced reality in my first years of parenting. That reality was that there were many issues on many levels I didn't have to address until I had children.

The most effective way I've found to reach my children's hearts has been to 1) **accept** the reality of who and where I *actually* am (or who and where my children *actually* are), 2) sincerely **ask** God for help with my own heart (rather than just asking Him to change their hearts), 3) learn to be still long enough to wait and **listen** to see if there's something I'm supposed to change or do, and 4) follow through on anything I've become aware of (**obey**).

It was tempting for me to want to bypass this painful process, and simply believe that giving my children the best meant to give them the best opportunities. When I saw others' young children excel in academics, music or sports, I became fearful that our children would be hindered if they bypassed those once-in-a-childhood opportunities. When I got caught up looking to the left or right at what others were doing, fears would creep in and I'd begin to lose my ability to judge correctly. Whenever I returned to looking to the Lord for direction, and to staying within my husband's direction, I could see that we'd chosen the best path for *our* children. Thus, I found that if I entertained comparison or fear, I was less able to obey God's direction for us.

Sometimes in pursuit of the best, we parents spend an inordinate amount of time taking younger children to say, a club meeting on Monday, dance class on Tuesday, violin on Wednesday and co-op on Thursday. By the time Friday rolls around Mom's energy reserves are drained from planning, chauffeuring, volunteering and preparing for the next meeting. We also begin to look like we're our children's servants rather than their parents!

There's a difference between pouring ourselves into young children which says, "You are important *to* me," and burning ourselves out for them which says "You are *more important than* me." Both lifestyles have high costs, but the high maintenance in working on character first can result in less effort later as the emotionally-healthy, more giving child develops.

Winning our child's heart isn't centering our homes around our child's wants and desires. Indulging a child's moods or allowing his *wants* to take precedence over his *needs* causes a child to grow up with the illusion that life revolves around him. When he goes out into the world of extended family, neighborhood, church, extra-curricular activity, ministry, job, college or career he'll face tension or conflicts because he's no longer the center of other people's worlds. We want to create Christ-centered, character-centered homes, not child-centered homes. We want to train our children in character because it's right for them to develop character, and to learn that the world, beginning with our home, doesn't revolve around them.

Winning our child's heart is not centering our homes around our children's character flaws or weaknesses. If children can slide from the standards or behavior set by their parents, they establish that in those areas they've become the center of the home. God rebuked Eli because he refused to rein in his sons when they were disobedient. By default, Eli created a child-centered home.[18] If we turn a blind eye when our children cheat in a game, exaggerate facts, take more than their share, or blame others for their conflicts, we build our homes around their sin. If we entertain thoughts that the whole world is against our child and he just needs our protection, we're hindering his character development. We have to be convinced that teaching our children to work with, think of and love others (beginning first in their own family) is mentally, emotionally and spiritually healthy for them.

Winning our child's heart is not excusing bad behavior for

the sake of peace. It's not adapting our behavior to please a difficult child, or asking family members to "tip-toe" around a sibling because he might react, or because it's easier to work around a child than to try to change him. There are times in every family when everyone bends for the one – when the one is facing additional trials. We all need to give each other some healthy room as we encounter life's rougher moments. That kind of flexibility is one of the attributes that makes the home a safe place. But if the exception becomes a way of life, or if we fail to set reasonable expectations on behavior, or if we don't administer consistent, reasonable consequences, we make it harder for a child to face his own responsibilities, himself, and one day – the outside world. We'll win his favor for the moment, but lose his respect and eventually his heart.

Winning our child's heart is not "going to bat" for him against the world when we think he's been unfairly treated. Of course, we protect our children from harm (whether physical, mental, emotional or spiritual), but how often in their trials we miss the opportunity to teach them a higher lesson, or a more mature life skill. Often, we want to fix the problem, and we totally miss the fact that some types of problems (and people) just never go away. Jesus said, "Tomorrow will have enough trouble of its own."[19] How wise if we teach our children first how to benefit when they're wronged. We can encourage them in faith and help them to see that God is bigger than whatever trials may come. We also want to help them understand that He is there to help

> We have to be convinced that teaching our children to work with, think of and love others is mentally, emotionally and spiritually healthy for them.

them with *responses*, and not necessarily their vindication or reward. Children should benefit from their trials, just as we adults are supposed to. They can be taught discretion in learning when to speak up for a cause and when to be silent. We can encourage them to call on the Lord first when they've been wronged. We can help them navigate through the waters of patience, mercy and forgiveness.

Life isn't going to be suddenly "fair" when they go out into the world, and learning how to deal with that fact is valuable training for adult life. But, oh, how much easier it is for them to find their way when they've watched us navigate through our own trials.

We don't have to be perfect parents to win our child's heart. There *are* no perfect parents as we (and they) know. Parents will disappoint and fail children, and children will disappoint and fail parents. But, if we excuse ourselves, blame others or resign ourselves to defeat when we fail, we miss the chance to show them what redemption looks like. Our job is to turn to that wonderfully perfect God when we fail, and in turning show them the way. That's one very important way they learn to trust Him.

...our own children's hearts before they become...

Becoming Fishers of ᵛ Men

Many years ago our family spent the weekend at a campground on the beach. Well after dark we took a walk to a bridge over Florida's Intracoastal Waterway. We were surprised by a large nightlife community of local fishermen crowded onto both sides of the bridge. Like a gawking tourist I found myself drawn to them, staring at a side of life that I never knew existed.

People actually left the comforts of home at that hour to stand for hours and hours, fishing from a bridge until the wee hours of the morning?

I was fascinated. I leaned over the bridge captivated by the scores of spidery, silvery lines being pulled taut by the current twenty feet below. Each shining line eerily caught the lights of the bridge and then disappeared into the dark, fast-moving water. How they kept them all from tangling I'll never know.

Suddenly, an old fisherman's pole bent sharply and he called. Immediately, nearby fishermen rallied to his aid. One or two offered advice. Another grabbed his own net and gave it to him. Some stepped aside to give him extra space to work his reel. I've never been good at fishing but I would have thrown in line and hook that night just to be a part of that tight circle of mutual good will, fun and support. We seemed like invisible outsiders watching a close-knit family tick.

I became absorbed in the fisherman's battle to bring in his catch. He was obviously a veteran and knew exactly what to do. Back and forth, in and out, reel in, wait, shift weight, reel in again, wait, shift again, reel in again and so on. It surprised me to see how much shifting and adjusting and changing the fisherman had to do to bring in his catch. It was so much work! Just for a fish? And it was slow work. So slow, in fact that I was tempted to offer my own advice. *Just reel the thing in and get it over with, will you?*

After ten long minutes a huge fish broke through the water. Another man began lowering his own rope and net to the surface to help bring it in, thinking the fish's weight might break the line. Finally, a large tarpon was flopping about the bridge and everyone gathered around to see and to slap the man on the back for a job well done.

On our walk back to camp I thought about why I wouldn't have been able to bring that fish in. I liked the camaraderie of the moment, but I didn't really want a fish. The fisherman did. He wanted a fish so much that he'd taken the time to learn the best way to catch one. He'd been patient and determined, yet he'd stayed flexible. I would love to have experienced the thrill of reeling in that fish, but I had neither his passion nor his willingness to learn. Had I grabbed his rod and reel after the hook was set, I would have probably still lost the fish. The right tools in my hands wouldn't have made me an expert. The right tools in his hands didn't make him an expert either. But, his willingness to learn, to adapt his methods, his flexibility with the line, and his patience to keep trying had made him into an expert.

Follow Me, and I will make you fishers of men. Matthew 4:19

If we want to build godly character in our children it helps to begin by reeling in the heart. Patiently, gently, but firmly, never giving up, even when the struggle is long. The tension on the line between fish and fisherman was constant and real.[20] That pressure sometimes forced the fisherman to flex and adjust. He flexed because he knew he'd lose the fish if he were rigid and unyielding.

> We earn the right to fish for other men's hearts by our obedience to fish first for hearts within our own families

I realize that the disciples used nets for fishing rather than line and hook, but a fisherman must learn the most effective ways to bring in fish. And just as we can understand giving by observing a seed grow,[21] maturity by watching a vine be pruned,[22] or evangelism by observing the harvest,[23] so we can learn about God's ways by observing those things around us. God has tucked many clues about Himself and His ways into the natural world that surrounds us. If we only had eyes to see!

For since the creation of the world, His invisible attributes are clearly seen, being understood by the things that are made. Romans 1:20

If we only work to win the hearts of those outside our homes (who are actually other people's children) but fail to win the hearts of our own children, we miss an important truth. It's only right that we win the hearts of those for whom we have primary responsibility before we take on the responsibilities of other men's hearts for the Lord. We actually earn the right to fish for other men's hearts by our obedience to fish first for hearts within our own families. Our family becomes the validation of further ministry, and a testimony to others of Jesus' power to change hearts and lives. When detailing the requirements for a pastor, Paul asks Timothy the rhetorical question, "For if a man does not know how to rule his own house, how shall he take care of the church of God?"[24] It's understood that one who wants to shepherd other people's hearts must first shepherd his own family's hearts. At home, and with our own children, is where we're all supposed to begin.

Why We Win Their Hearts

There are parents who have done an excellent job winning their children's hearts, but because they have never met the Lord themselves, they haven't led their children to Him. How much is lost if we gain our children's hearts but never help them to know the Lord. We have an awesome responsibility to use our influence, once we've won their hearts, to lead them to the Savior.

The How-Tos of It

So, how do we, in the day-to-day interacting with our children, go about winning their hearts and keeping that oneness of fellowship? Many of the lessons we learned were simply common sense. But in the parent-child relationship the obvious can become clouded by needs and hurt and emotions.

Gain Their Trust

There are many ways to earn and keep our children's trust, but there are even more ways to lose it. I've made the mistake of sharing the details of our children's struggles with other parents here and there, only to discover later that my words had been overheard, or repeated back to my children, and that my children felt embarrassed and somewhat betrayed. Needless to say, I had to ask forgiveness and regain some of the trust I had lost.

There *are* times that it helps to ask counsel from another parent who has faced (and overcome) similar conflicts with their children, or to seek counsel from grandparents, minister or counselor when we're truly stumped. But, sharing too many details, especially with those who've had no experience, or sharing out of frustration can make it hard to keep our children's trust.

If our children feel they can't be vulnerable and open with us, if they don't think their sins are confidential and safe with us, they'll be less likely to share their hearts with us in the future.

Earn Respect with Consistent Boundaries

On the one hand we need to train our children to respect us (based on our right to have them respect us), while on the other hand respect really has to be earned. No one gives their heart to someone they don't respect. It's true that people give their hearts to people they *shouldn't* respect. But, the fact is that they do respect them; they just respect them for the wrong reasons.

A child's heart can't be truly won without winning their respect. One of the most fundamental ways to gain respect is by establishing firm boundaries and giving consistent consequences (without anger) for wrong behavior.

Earn Respect with Consistent Living

Respect will also be earned as they observe how we live our own lives, and by our own lack of duplicity.

Earn Respect by Treating Them with Respect

We can try to teach a child to respect us, but unless we also treat him with respect, he may comply on the outside but find it difficult to give true respect from the inside. Even though it takes more time, it's actually more efficient to make the effort to teach respect by our example.

Common courtesies such as saying "please" and "thank you," listening without interrupting, trying to understand a situation before trying to "fix" it, giving the benefit of the doubt (unless he's broken our trust and shows that he needs accountability), and giving correction softly and privately are the basics in respect and good manners. Behaviors that erode respect would be resignation, bargaining, bribing, berating, manipulating, whining, complaining, crying, comparing, threatening or imploring.

Being a busy mom of many young children I was always looking for ways to "kill several birds with one stone." But, if I try to be too efficient when dealing with children, I kill relationships instead of those proverbial birds. I also had a strong personality, and was usually able to get my children to comply on the outside, only later realizing that I had damaged them on the inside.

While multiple-bird-killing-techniques work well for paperwork and housework, they don't work well when dealing with people. I'm ashamed to say that too many times I was more considerate of the feelings of friends (or even strangers) than of my own children.

Confess Faults

When we make a mistake, when we over-discipline, when we sin against them or offend, the fastest way to regain credibility and solid ground again is to quickly admit our fault. Without justifying or excusing, without blaming anyone or anything else, we just admit we were wrong.

I have often excused my sin by saying things like, "Yes, I yelled at you (or over-corrected you, or was impatient with you, or forgot my promise), but I have been up all night with the baby (or have had morning sickness, or am overtired, or have been so busy)." However, it wasn't long before I began to hear our children excusing their sin by saying things like, "Yes, I hit him (or was mean to him, or didn't finish my work, or cheated in the game), but he hit me first (or he took my toy, or I just don't feel good, or I'm in a bad mood today). I had been setting an example and had begun to reap the consequences in reproduced behaviors and excuses. When I began to say, "I was so wrong to yell at you, and you are so important to me. I'm so sorry I overreacted to what you did. Would you please forgive me?" I began teaching them how to forgive, not through a lesson-plan or Bible study on forgiveness – but through my own example.

Admitting our faults to our children not only keeps walls

from going up between their hearts and ours, it teaches them by example how to admit their own faults. We don't expect them to "get over it" without our making things right if we offend. They are the weaker brethren.[25]

Of course, we use discretion and don't confess sins to our children that are inappropriate or if they weren't directly involved, "Mommy did a bad thing today and called Mrs. Higgenbotham a nosy, uninformed, ugly, old gossip after she told the neighbors that you would be socially-impaired if we homeschooled you, and *I am very sorry!*" And we don't subject children to unnecessary details of adult issues, "Mommy was so wrong to call Uncle Harmon's estranged wife a sorry pin-head when she asked Daddy to post bail for her abusive, live-in lover's, ex-con step-son, and *I am very sorry!*" There is an appropriate time to learn about adult issues (and that time is different with each child), but once children are exposed to them there is no return.

> If I try to be too efficient with children, I kill relationships instead of those proverbial birds.

Bring Correction Privately, and Not While Emotions are High

If we correct children for their sin, or point out their faults when either their emotions or ours are running hot, it will be hard for them to respond correctly. Strong emotions usually signal that people feel deeply about something and want to be heard, accepted, understood, defended or vindicated. While we must enforce consequences for bad behavior during a conflict, it's much more effective to wait until after the conflict is over to try to show them their error.

Our own children tend to be much more open to chat about heart issues near bedtime. Sometimes I'd replay a conflict, or help younger ones to role-play.

Listening to their complaints about each other privately, out of the other's earshot, was extremely helpful. I absorbed some of the angry feelings, charged words, or assumed motivations which would have further damaged their relationship with that sibling. I could try to identify with their hurt, and hopefully bring them to forgiveness before coaching them on how to bring a complaint to their sibling. I didn't always do it the same way, and I didn't always do it "right." Sometimes I brought the complaint back to the sibling for them, sometimes I jumped to conclusions after hearing the first account, and sometimes I misjudged their motivations. But, by listening privately to complaints I was able to head off even more damage. It's like becoming the liver in the body of Christ, filtering out the toxins and then releasing back into the system only that which is profitable to the body. It's much easier for a parent to sift through harsh feelings and words and get to the root of the problem, than for a sibling to hear complaints that are missed with emotion.

Commend Them More

It was hard to believe the difference that began to happen in the dynamics of our home when I began to commend our children more. Praise (encouraging them while it's called Today) is such an effective way to win their hearts that we've written an entire chapter on it.

Learn to Listen

It's important to talk to our children about the things that really matter in life, but I think it may be more important to listen.

I used to think that listening involved taking in every detail of every description of every subject from every child. But, with seven children there was so much talk at our house that I began to experience "input overload." I've since learned that I can filter out a lot of words and still detect attitudes and needs. I had to learn to listen with less intensity if the inflection is factual and routine, with more interest if there is enthusiasm and excitement, and with a drop-everything-and-I-am-all-yours focus if there is offense, misunderstanding, anger, sorrow or genuine need.

Listening is where real living takes place, where feelings are shared, hearts open up, lives bond, courses are changed and maybe even history is made. Listening to our children is something that should take precedence over our schedule. It's so important to listen to our children.

Try to "Come Alongside"

I also found that whenever I could shift my position in a confrontation, even just bit, to a place of coming alongside to listen, understand and support, that the end result was less conflicts and ultimatums. That doesn't mean that parents will never have conflicts or have to issue ultimatums if they're more understanding, but tension definitely decreases when empathy increases. If we can get a hold of the truth that we're on the same path together, that we've felt the same feelings, made the same mistakes (and even made worse mistakes) we earn the right to instruct. This position doesn't diminish our authority as parents; it gives us credibility. We're not surrendering our authority to our children; we're allowing our children to identify with us, so they'll trust us to help them more. It's a subtle difference in our attitude, but can make such a big impact.

Give Them Some "Space" and Opportunities for Self-Government

This is not the same as letting children work out their own conflicts. When children are left to "work it out on their own" without the guidance of a caring adult, the skills they acquire rarely have much to do with justice, equity or righteousness. Sadly, their social skills will often be reduced to who is smarter, faster or bigger. They're children. They're immature. We are adults who are supposed to help give them direction based on good judgment. Children need wise "judges" until they can judge themselves rightly.

> Giving our children opportunities for self-government provides "test-runs" that are beneficial for transition into adulthood.

Giving them space involves letting them begin to make some of their own decisions within safe boundaries. For example, as children become more self-governing they can be given some (and eventually most) of their responsibilities and assignments on a weekly or monthly basis, and some freedom of choosing how and when to work on each assignment (as long as they don't conflict with other family commitments).

Sometimes they'll make mistakes with that freedom and procrastinate on their least favorite subject until the last minute. As long as we let them begin self-government in small steps, and we've given reasonable expectations and consequences, then we want to let them fail (without nagging or reminding), and then suffer their own consequences.

As children succeed in being faithful with smaller steps they earn the right (and responsibility) of more freedoms. Not only is this encouraging to them to be given more trust and freedom with their own schedule (i.e.: life) but it shifts their responsibility (and reaction when they fail) away from us, back to the schedule and to whatever consequences we've set. We shift from nagging to a less emotionally-invested evaluation of our children's growing maturity.

Giving our children opportunities for self-government provides incremental "test-runs" that are so beneficial for transition into adulthood.

Tell Them How Very Special They Are

One of our teens has a favorite saying: "You're unique. Just like everyone else!" How true that is. Think of how each piece of a jigsaw puzzle is uniquely cut, designed by its creator to fill a very special place in the overall picture. Each piece has a unique, very special position, with its own part of the picture displayed on it. When every piece of the puzzle finds its place, the eye is drawn to the beauty of the picture. If some pieces don't find their place, the eye is drawn to the holes and the whole picture suffers.

Our children need to hear over and over (and over and over and over) that they are very special to God, very special to us, and a very special part of a bigger picture. Helping them to understand how special they are can help them rise above some of the smaller issues that bog people down, and give them a positive vision about their role in the world, beginning in our home.

Parents also tell children how special they are by touch. Our family tends to hug a lot, and our teens have always enjoyed hugs, but some teens may feel awkward with physical closeness for a while. Even then, a hand on the shoulder, or on an arm, especially at bedtime when the pace tends to slow a little and when there is more time for feelings, can be very important.

Let Them Be Children

Being a child is different from *acting* like a child. Acting like a child means acting immaturely, which is something that we expect children to do, but we don't reward. Being a child means having time to play. Of course, playing is something to be enjoyed after studies and responsibilities are completed – or playtime has to become "finish those studies and responsibilities time." But a child should never have so many studies and responsibilities that he can't reasonably finish in time to enjoy some rest and play.

Being a child also means not being burdened with a tightly-packed schedule and high-pressure expectations. And it means being free to enjoy just being a child without the weight of adult issues until they're closer to becoming adults.

Never Give Up!

It takes a lot of energy to parent. At first it's mostly physical energy, but it gradually shifts to more mental, emotional and spiritual energy. It also takes energy to win and keep (or to regain and keep) our children's hearts. When we get tired or discouraged we can feel like giving up.

During those times we have to remind ourselves that God loves to do the impossible. All we have to do is ask. I know how hard it is to pray when discouraged. A stony, weary, discouraged heart doesn't *want* to pray! When my thoughts get negative, I have to force myself to pray out loud.

I encourage you to pray out loud rather than just in your heart. God does hear the prayers of our hearts, but He also tells us to call on Him, and David writes that the Lord delivered him when He cried to Him with his voice. God may send gentle wisdom, gentle comfort or gentle chastening. But, He *will* answer if you call. Never, never give up.

If your child is already an adult, and you feel you'll never be able to win his heart back, be encouraged. The most important thing is that our children one day come to know the Lord. That is ultimately why we seek their hearts. Ask God every day to send other people to win your child to Him. And stay open to any correction or opportunities the Lord may help you to see.

Winning our child's heart *is* a bit like learning to fish with hook and line. Our job is to take our place on that bridge and learn what it takes to draw them in. We brace ourselves for resistance, ready to hold firm so the fish won't be lost, while at the same time we're prepared to give a short release if the line gets too tight, so the fish won't be lost. Sometimes the tension will mean we need to shift in position, sometimes it will mean they need to yield in theirs. One interaction at time we're getting to know the Lord better, ourselves better and our children better. And like fishing community, we try to help one another when we can, and rejoice when another succeeds. We're becoming fishers of men.

Chapter Three: Get to the Root of the Problem

The measure of a man's real character is what he would do if he knew he would never be found out.   Lord McCaulay

When a child doesn't perform well academically, is it always a competency problem or could it be a lack of character? When he drags his feet on assignments, daydreams during math, or continually makes the same mistakes, is it always a character problem or could it be a lack of competency? If he dislikes reading, but loves to play, has no patience with grammar, but can draw cartoons or stack toys for long periods, is it immaturity or could it be a lack of character? If we can't seem to motivate him, or find the key to inspire him, or get him to concentrate, is the problem with the child, or with the curriculum or with us?

> The first step in finding the answer for each child is asking the Lord for help.

Our family has experienced all these scenarios, and all these answers, to a greater or lesser degree with one child or another at one time or another.

The first step in finding the answer for each child has been to admit to the Lord that I needed help. This sounds incredibly simple but I'm ashamed of how many times I've overlooked the obvious. There's a huge difference between discussing with friends, other parents, grandparents or an evaluator the fact that I can't figure out why a child isn't performing well, or spending large amounts of time researching what I think may be his problem – and seriously and consistently asking God for wisdom to help that child.

That's not to say we don't find help by asking for counsel or doing research. But answers have amazingly "dropped into our laps" when I called out to God first for our children's needs. Sometimes the search for the answer and the waiting for wisdom is a short time; sometimes it's longer. The key is in to not give up asking the Lord for help and wisdom.

Character Weakness vs. Personal Uniqueness

Once we've sincerely asked the Lord for wisdom, it helps to evaluate a child's academic performance in light of other behaviors. If a child is trying to please us in every other area, then poor academic performance probably isn't a character issue. If he makes his bed, does his chores, and takes on other requests without cutting corners – but he's balking in math or daydreaming while he's supposed to be reading, the answer is probably something we can change for him rather than forcing him to change.

Perhaps the material is too advanced and he's frustrated or he feels resigned. Perhaps it's too easy and he's bored. Maybe he's an auditory learner and he doesn't comprehend material well when he has to read silently. He could be a right-brain dominant child who will blossom academically later in adolescence. He might have any number of disabilities of which we aren't yet aware such as dyslexia, weak vision or impaired hearing. Perhaps he's not emotionally mature enough for the amount of time he's being asked to study. He could be academically-delayed or not be ready scholastically for his grade level.

These scenarios aren't character problems but just uniquenesses that we need to accept in order to help our child. (More on understanding uniqueness in the next chapter.)

If a child's character is growing and healthy but he lags in academics, we want to tweak the curriculum to the ability and needs of the child, not force the child to comply with the format or schedule of a particular curriculum. We want to teach the *child,* not the *curriculum.*

This is where a veteran evaluator can be very helpful. They might recognize a problem by the symptoms we describe. Perhaps they've seen or used another curriculum which might be better suited for the way our child learns. They might be able to refer us to another parent who has experienced that child's rate of development, or to an author who is familiar with his learning style, or to a professional who can help with a special need. They may even be able to suggest certain types of testing to determine a specific problem. Local groups are also a good source for tapping into experienced help. And curriculum suppliers, the educational community at large, the local library and the Internet are all packed with how-tos and helpful books on various learning styles and needs.

Character Weakness in Academics and Other Areas

However, if we see a child displaying negative character traits in other areas, those traits are most assuredly affecting his academics. If he's prone to laziness (keeps choosing the easiest path), if he's concerned mostly with pleasing himself, if he tends to whine and complain when asked to do reasonable chores, or he displays bad attitudes toward others, those are character problems that will also show up in academics.

Changing the curriculum won't solve a character problem. It can even mask a character problem. There's a difference between a child saying, in effect, "I don't *want* to finish that lesson (or read that story or memorize those facts)," and a child who is developmentally struggling to learn in a certain way or on a certain timetable.

And what if our child excels academically but displays problems like willfulness, pride, lying, stealing, stubbornness or rebellion? What if he's diligent with his studies but careless with his words? The champion in his competitions but more concerned with his performance than with his conscience or his relationships? Should working with him on those problems take precedence over academic advancement?

If it's a character problem, we're wasting time if we just whack at bad fruit ("Stop doing that!"), but don't pull up the root ("Honey, let's talk about why you're doing that.")

It's tempting to overlook our children's wrong attitudes or behavior. We may feel ill-equipped to help them, so we avoid the problem. Or we tell ourselves their behavior is a stage, or that it's normal, or that it will pass. We might be tempted to keep them busy in extra-curricular activities as diversions until they "get through a phase." Sometimes we just don't see how we can find the time to address attitudes.

If we don't first consider root causes, we run the risk of burying the true problems and postponing the inevitable. If a child is displaying weak character when he's ten, those problems won't just go away when he becomes an adolescent. Adolescence is a time of harvest, usually producing bumper crops of either good fruit or bad. And the longer they grow, the harder they are to remove once we finally decide to face them.

> To allow sins to grow unchecked is like saying we don't have time to pull weeds when we see them coming up in our garden.

But we only have our children with us for a few years! To allow sins and weaknesses to grow unchecked is like deciding we don't have time to pull weeds when we see them coming up in our garden. If we don't take care of that garden while it's in our stewardship, if our children don't learn to "judge themselves rightly"26 before they leave our home, the Master Gardener will have to prune them Himself once they're on their own. Those lessons are usually more difficult. Our children's future professors and bosses won't be as invested in them, as forgiving or as understanding as we are. They'll be enrolling in a school of hard knocks that usually include a few trips to our Father's heavenly woodshed (He chastens those whom He loves27 and trials can be a form of chastening).28 It works; it's just easier on them if we can help them overcome some of their sins while they're young.

The home is much more conducive to dealing with character development than the world. Parents are the first to see sins as they sprout, so we have a special opportunity to help them nip them in the bud.

The Momzilla Meter

We just want to make sure we nip weeds and not hearts. Our anger isn't the same as righteous anger, even though it may feel like it when we see our children doing wrong. Jesus got very angry, but He was angry with people who said they spoke for His Father, but then misrepresented Him, "laying burdens on men's shoulders that were hard to bear."29 They made it harder for people to reach His Father. The Apostle Paul also vented anger and harsh words on people, but again, only on people who said they were speaking for God and then misrepresented Him demanding that people keep more laws than the message of grace required.30

It can be tempting to get angry when our child's besetting sin is the same as ours. A parent can become fearful and intolerant – or overly tolerant and blasé, using their own failure as an excuse for their child. As for me, each child made me feel like our home was turning into a carnival of fun house "mirrors," each one reflecting one problem or another in my own life. Only I wasn't having any fun.

Anger damages. It can be debilitating on many levels. Praying was the *last* thing I wanted to do when I was angry. Many times I forced a desperate prayer.

Help, Lord Jesus! I'm so angry and I really want to explode. And, by the way, I don't feel like praying, either! But, right now, I give You permission to work on my heart. Show me anything that I need to see, or anything I need to surrender to You.

There were plenty of times I didn't turn to the Lord and reaped the bad fruit of anger. Even when I did turn to the Lord I didn't always feel better right away. But there was often a tiny wisp of grace available once I prayed so I could get through the moment without sin.

I soon learned to rank my negative feelings on the imaginary, but very real "Momzilla Meter." I also began to understand that if someone could do something that caused me to peg out at "10," there was a lesson *I* was also supposed to be learning.

Rules, Standards and Consequences

That doesn't mean that because we start focusing on our own hearts that we no longer enforce boundaries for our children. Decisions about rules, standards and appropriate consequences need to be decided ahead of time. Consistent consequences establish a healthy feeling of security and supply outward pressure to conform.

It's not character strength that tolerates disrespectful words or attitudes in our children; it's weakness. Just as we put fences around young children to keep them from being hurt, so we place rules around the immature. We don't expect a two-year old to stay inside the yard simply because we explained to him the truth that cars are dangerous. Then the rules we placed on him (such as holding our hand when he crosses the street) will no longer apply. He'll govern himself without the need for rules in that area.

Truth never changes, but rules do. We want to teach our children how to live by truth, but until they do we place them under rules with consequences to protect them. We just want to be careful to administer those consequences in the right spirit.

We need to ask the Lord to help us to bring both truth and love to our children, and to know when to give more truth and accountability, and when to show more mercy. It's not easy. Apart from the Holy Spirit giving us discernment and wisdom, it's impossible!

> If we use the Bible as a club, it's unlikely that our children will allow it to get close enough to their hearts to cut between soul and spirit.

Once I pray for that child and check my own heart, I can approach him with my concerns. If I do this slowly (as in one character problem at a time so as not to overwhelm him), and in a private, gentle way, I can often help him see the problem.

If he has already received Jesus Christ as his Savior, then we can remind him that just as he asked for mercy to be saved, he can also ask for mercy and help in time of need. If he hasn't yet received the Lord, we need to remind ourselves that without the Holy Spirit working in his heart he'll be powerless to truly change. He may be especially miserable and reactionary if he's beginning to understand that himself, but hasn't yet yielded to God.

He also needs to know that everyone faces struggles and needs, and that everyone is in the same boat, and must ask the Lord to truly change their hearts. This is "inward drawing" – showing him what's right and appealing to him (in love) to change from the inside.

It helps a great deal if he knows that my interest is in him, that I truly want him to do what's right because it's best for him to do so, and not because his nonconformance is disrupting my life and our household (even though it may be). But the only way that he can know this to be true – *is if it is true.* If it's not true, I can *tell* him that my interest is primarily in his benefit, but he will *know* that it's not. My attitude and reactions will eventually reveal my true intentions.

We have learned, however, not to use Scripture study or memorization as a consequence to wrong behavior (*Honey, you've been lazy lately, so I'd like you to memorize two verses about the sloth.*). That is similar to whacking a patient with the flat side of the surgeon's knife. The Great Physician is able to cut through to root problems in the heart with the double-edged sword of the Spirit – if we gently lead them at teachable moments. But if we use Scripture as a club, it's unlikely they'll allow it to get close enough to their hearts to cut between soul and spirit.[31]

In most marriages the dad is better at designing outward pressure and the mom is good at drawing in her children's hearts. But, if the mother expects her husband to be good at winning their hearts also, so that each parent is then equally balanced in their approach to their children, she will be frustrated. In marriage, a balance is often found *between* the parents, not equally *in* each parent, so that one's strengths offset the other's limitations. In addition, if a wife strives against her husband it will be more likely that her children will strive against her and/or their father. A child's heart will be divided in a house divided against itself.

In a few marriages the mother is very good at designing outward pressure while her husband is good at drawing in the children's hearts. That fact doesn't mean that he can't lead; it means he can lead first in winning their hearts – if she will let him. She'll need wisdom to yield her expectations of how she thought their parenting would look to the Lord. She'll want to honor her husband's strengths and accept and balance out some of his weaknesses. How difficult it will be for her to win her children's respect if she doesn't respect her husband. And how much easier she'll find parenting if she learns to accept her husband's differences, and appreciate his strengths.

The principal relationship in the home is the marriage. If this relationship is suffering, relationships with our children will suffer. All the truths we apply to winning our children's hearts are even truer with a spouse: we try to win their hearts through keeping our word, admitting when we're wrong and giving kindness and respect.

If We Don't Have Our Child's Heart

If we don't have our child's heart – if he isn't open to us or to our instruction or correction, if he doesn't respond to our praise, if he's more concerned with pleasing himself than he is with pleasing us – then it gets more difficult (but even more important) to get to the root of the problem.

For our family and for many families we've heard from, unforgiveness is a very real hurdle to reaching our children's hearts. In many ways our children are the "weaker brethren" of Romans 14.

If they are to learn how to walk in forgiveness, they need to be shown how to do it through the mature examples of those they love and trust. But, if they are hurt by us, especially if those hurts have been overlooked or never forgiven, they'll put up a wall to keep us out. If they reject us, they'll reject our message and our efforts to help them. This rejection often doesn't show up until the teen years. One major reason (but not the only reason) that our children close their hearts to us is because of past hurts.

One summer I took the children to an old cabin in the mountains for a few weeks where Bill was going to join us after the workweek. Our ten-year old's attitude was terrible. He dragged his feet when I asked him for anything, snapped at his siblings, "misunderstood" even the simplest requests and was making life difficult for all of us. Early on our first night, after several warnings and then confrontations, I sent him to bed. But, my conscience panged me. It wasn't the way that I wanted our vacation to begin and I felt helpless to get through to him. After the younger children were tucked in, I dropped to my knees in my room and cried out to the Lord.

Lord, I'm so grieved over the separation that I sense between my son and me. I love him so much! I would do anything to help him. He means the world to me! How can I bridge the gap that I sense developing between us? I hate to see his heart begin to drift away!

After I finished pouring out my heart, I quietly waited, still on my knees. After a few moments, I had a clear thought.

*Why don't you tell **him** those things you just prayed?*

What? I thought. *Tell **him**?*

I'm ashamed now to recall how scary that idea was to me. I worried that if I told him how special and wonderful he was when he was behaving so badly that it would give him license to act even worse. It's also shameful for me to say that I couldn't remember the last time I had genuinely praised him for who he was. But we had talked every day!

What, I wondered, <u>*had*</u> *I been saying to him every day?* I replayed the words that had filled the last few days.

"No, Honey, please don't do that."
"Honey, we've already talked about that, remember?"
"I don't want to have to talk to you about that again."
"You know the consequences."
"Why are you doing that?!"
"Honey, stop!"
"Stop!"

I'd only been praying a short time but my heart was aching. I tiptoed to his room, and finding him awake asked if he would like to join me for hot chocolate. (I was sweetening the deal, thinking he might decline.) Over steaming cups of chocolate I told him exactly what had happened – what I'd prayed for him, and how I realized that I rarely bothered to tell him how much I really cared for him.

And then I told him the truth: that I was so sad over the separation I sensed between us, that he meant the world to me, that he was very special in so many ways, that I didn't tell him enough how much I loved him and that I wanted to bridge the gap that I sensed developing between us. His countenance changed and he began to soften. I asked his forgiveness which he readily gave.

As we sat there talking I took another chance at a risky question. Had I done anything else to offend him? When he quickly answered "No," I felt a little relieved, but mostly I was unconvinced. So heady with fresh insight and with a new communication between us (and with chocolate and caffeine pulsating through my veins), I threw pride to the wind and bravely rephrased the question.

"Well, if you could change anything in our home or in your life, what do you think you would change?" When I saw his brow furrow, I added, "You can share anything at all. I really want to know."

"Well," he slowly began, "I feel like you hold me to a higher standard than everyone else. You're harder on me than the others."

Plunk. That was the sound of an arrow of truth hitting my already wounded heart. And *clunk* – the sound of my pride hitting the floor as it struck.

I sensed he was testing the waters with this comment and needed to know if it was safe, so I made up my mind that I wouldn't try to defend myself or try to "fix" him in any way. I decided to listen. I tossed out all the defense arguments that had already begun filing into the courtroom of my mind, and feeling somewhat like a masochist asked for more.

> I told him the truth: that I was sad over the separation between us, that I loved him, that he meant the world to me, that he was very special, and that I didn't tell him enough how much I loved him.

"What else, Sweetheart?" I squeaked.

After a short pause he threw out another grievance. Then another, and another until all of his known hurts and offenses, along with (what I thought at the time was) the rest of my pride, were gone.

I took a deep breath and reviewed his list. On the one hand, it was consoling to realize that over half of it was exaggerated – the result of a child's immature perspective, seen through the eyes of hurts and unforgiveness. On the other hand, I was concerned about his response if I defended myself. I decided to overlook them for the moment and address the ones that had hit the target of guilt in my heart.

"You know, you're right about many of these things. I *have* been harder on you. And I see that I've been wrong to do that. I wish I could turn back the clock and change my actions so that you wouldn't have suffered these hurts. Would you please forgive me?"

I can't describe the joy that filled my heart that night as a wall of separation between my child and me began to crumble. I had become dull to the pangs of guilt, excusing myself because of my busyness and feelings of inability to do anything about it.

Of course, that night was not the end of our struggles, but it marked a change in direction for our family. I asked him to make a commitment to me that if anything hurt or offended him in the future, that he would bring it to me before the end of the day. I, in turn, made a commitment to him that when he brought something to me, that I would stop and listen. We didn't always keep those commitments, but each time we did, it brought more good fruit. He also told us many years later that the events of that night were a turning point for him in many of his personal struggles because he felt that he had been truly heard and understood for the first time in a long time.

Unforgiveness

In Matthew 18 Jesus tells a parable about a man who, though forgiven much by the king, refused to forgive the smaller debts owed to him. When the king heard of his smallness of heart, he had him thrown into prison to be tormented. Jesus said, "*So shall my Heavenly Father do to you if you do not forgive your brother from your heart.*"

This harsh sentence always seemed hard for me to accept, until I began to really walk in forgiveness. I realized that unforgiveness is a prison cell and the handle to cell door is on the *inside*. I could get out of prison whenever I turned the handle. All I had to do was forgive. Once I walked out of my own prison and started functioning out from under the negative energy that I was used to, my eyes were opened to how much of my life I had actually spent "in the pokey." That experience made it much easier for me to recognize when my children were in their own prisons of unforgiveness. I could testify to them of the "tortures" of mind and soul that plague the unforgiving heart.

The moment we nurse an offense we check ourselves into a prison of expectations, hurts and unforgiveness. Almost immediately we see the people who hurt us with a very narrow view. The eyes of our heart perform a scan that somehow magnifies their bad points and overlooks their good ones. Even if that person's qualities are brought to our attention, they seem insignificant. If we don't completely forgive them, it's impossible to see them correctly. Motives come into question, intentions are misunderstood and their transgression becomes "the truth." Everything (including eventually our view of the world) becomes overshadowed by their offense. As an "ex-con," I can confidently assure my children that this is not a place they want to "do time."

One day I was listening to one of our children explain why he was so mad at his brother. As he went on I could just imagine that invisible prison cell of unforgiveness that surrounded him. There, standing firmly on his rights, inside of his own bars of expectations and offense, stood my son, as I had stood so many times before. I tried to patiently listen, giving him time to express his hurts before trying to show him the cell. Like me, I knew he was blinded by his hurts and didn't even know he was in prison. I tenderly showed him Matthew 18 and silently prayed that the Lord would soften his heart. I was going to tell him about the handle being on the inside of the cell door, but I found myself telling him instead that there was no door on *his* cell at all! There was, instead, an opening at the very bottom of his cell, big enough for him to crawl through. But he would have to climb down off of his stack of rights, and go very low – humble himself – to get out. It was such an amazing picture in my mind – we humans placing ourselves into prisons, blind to the bars that surround us, and living there day after day, year after year with an open door at our feet. If we could only "see," we would *want* to get out. And bowing low to crawl through a perfectly open door would seem like nothing at all just to be free.

Whether our prison door has its handle on the inside of the door, or has no door at all, we still must humble ourselves and release others before we can be free. Our son accepted the fact that he was in prison that day and prayed with me to surrender his rights – not, as he feared, to his brother – but safely to the Lord. He was then able to forgive his brother from his heart. He chocked up some valuable experience that day in being able to forgive someone before they repented, an important skill that he would need to rely on later when he faced offenses outside our family. Later, I talked privately to his brother about his behavior. What a difference it made in the rest of our day, and I know is continuing to make in the rest of that child's life.

It always makes us feel vulnerable to forgive someone, but once we do there's a freedom and a cleanness of heart that washes over the soul and buffers the fear of the next offense. One fear I battled that night at the cabin was that my son would give me a long list of grievances, and that by asking him what those grievances were I'd be allowing him to place me on trial. The truth was that he already had a list of grievances and that I had already been placed on trial. My not knowing what those grievances were didn't make them not exist! I had already been tried and judged – *but my son had been sent to prison*. Asking him to let me hear his hurts was my first step in helping him to get out. It was an awkward, risky shift in position for me since my imagination envisioned complaints such as, "I don't have enough privileges," or, "You shouldn't make me do my chores." My experience, though, has been that once real hurts are dealt with, and the real need of the heart for acceptance is met, there's more willingness to cooperate, not less.

Past hurts, whether they stem from broken promises, misunderstandings, over-correction, or even where no genuine offense exists except in the mind of the child, produce such a common root of unforgiveness that we do well if we talk to our children about how to recognize it and pull it out. It may seem small to us, but a hurt always appears bigger to the one who's been hurt. Children can't help but drag their feet, resist our help or stop achieving when they have old hurts settling in the bottoms of their hearts. Teaching our children how to yield their rights to the Lord and to walk in forgiveness is vital to their character growth and emotional health. But how helpless I was to show them until I had gained experience (not just head knowledge) going after that root in my own heart!

> I had already been tried and judged, but my son had been sent to prison.
>
> Asking him to let me hear his grievances was my first step in helping him to get out.

It's so important to identify the root of a problem in our children. We have to be willing to call sins by their proper names such as ungratefulness or discontentment instead of excusing them as being fussy or tired. I've sometimes missed an opportunity to lead our children through an open door of forgiveness because I excused a wrong attitude as waking up on the wrong side of the bed, or as just having a bad day instead of gently prodding for an offense. Teaching our children how to forgive is so helpful in avoiding root problems of bitterness. And when we "connect" them to eternal truths that then become theirs, they usually begin to trust us for more counsel.

Chapter Four: Understand and Accept Uniqueness

I will praise you for I am fearfully and wonderfully made.
Marvelous are your works! This my soul knows very well.
Psalms 139:14

Temperaments[32]

When our daughter was about ten we noticed that each time we planned an event or initiated any change that involved her or the family in general, she was quick to point out potential problems with it. She also asked for small details about the event that seemed irrelevant to me. It felt like she was passively challenging my authority with her questions. In her defense, she was obedient and would cooperate with whatever we decided. But, it felt like she had "set up camp" on the negative side of life, often concerned about problems that might never happen. It got to the point that if I planned something as simple as a field trip to the zoo, I would anticipate her quiet dissent in my mind before I even mentioned the trip.

One day I read that the some of the traits of the perfectionist Melancholy temperament included being a "hound for detail" with a unique ability to analyze a project and pinpoint its potential problems. I realized I had misjudged my daughter's motivation, and that she'd been operating out of strength, not challenging me out of rebellion or negativism. She really was a more cautious person, able to see obstacles more clearly than her Choleric/Sanguine mother who focused on achieving the goal and then having fun.

Once I understood her, I no longer felt challenged by her. I accepted the fact that she was the type of person who needed detail. I was also able to show her how to phrase her concerns so she wouldn't be perceived so negatively. I even saw the benefit of running things by her from time to time to let her help troubleshoot some of my quickly though-out plans.

Understanding the various ways our children think, learn, or see themselves and the world is not a magic formula that will solve all our communication problems or all their learning obstacles. But it certainly helps. Often their differences are really strengths that we don't recognize or understand, and not character flaws as I have sometimes presumed.

Other times their differences *were* character flaws, and being able to point out potential pitfalls and consequences within their unique strength or gift saved them frustration and heartache. It has also kept me from trying to force a "round child" into my idea of what a square "character mold" was supposed to look like *(Kate's cautious outlook must be a character flaw)*, or to compare them with their siblings or others' children *(Suzie has faced many more challenges than Kate, but has accepted them with a cheerful attitude, so Suzie must have more character than Kate)*. It has also helped our children to calibrate their viewpoints with truth *(Honey, even though you'll be uncomfortable with these changes, the Lord is still working all these things together for your good)*. While our children's responses within their temperaments can easily *become* character flaws *(Kate has now developed a critical attitude and is inwardly resistant to us)*, we gain great footage in helping them to overcome them if we can understand them.

Attitudes are the fruit of an inner viewpoint (and conclusions arrived at from those different vantage points), and not the root itself. Understanding various vantage points and viewpoints, then, is a great asset.

Four basic temperaments, **Choleric**, **Melancholy**, **Phlegmatic** and **Sanguine** were first documented in medieval times.[33]   When I first read about them I saw a humorous glimpse of each temperament displayed in the *Winnie the Pooh*[34] characters of Rabbit, Eyore, Pooh and Tigger. Eyore's "What if the glass is half-empty?"[35] outlook was what I had been reacting to in our daughter.

Our "Tigger," an incurably happy Sanguine, has enthusiastically (but innocently) bounced through every one of his sibling's "carrot patches" over the years (and a few of his parents'), leaving trails of offense behind. So, when this talkative, lively child, whose behavior is to act first/think later (if at all), seemed to be "flying off the handle" at the smallest thing, it seemed outrageous to all of us. I spent untold hours worrying about what we could have done wrong to produce such an easily-angered child! That was until I read that the Sanguine's bright, highly-verbal and highly-social nature can explode in sudden outbursts of anger, which he then quickly forgets all about!   Understanding his temperament weaknesses didn't excuse his anger *(That's just the way he is)*; it gave us insight into common pitfalls of his temperament so he could learn to avoid them. Letting him read about his own strengths and weaknesses also reassured him that he was facing the same temptations others do, and that he also had strengths that were special and important and different than his siblings'.

> Letting them read about their temperaments reassured them they were facing the same temptations others do, and that their strengths were different than their siblings.

Then there was our Phlegmatic laid-back, "Pooh" who seemed to have only one gear – first! But his personality was so easy-going, and his character so solid that we hesitated making him dig deep to see if there was a "second-gear" in there somewhere. After all, he would do most anything we asked – eventually! I had just about resigned myself to the idea that he was the "stop and smell the roses" type who would never develop ulcers, and that perhaps we should all be taking some life cues from him, when we read that two of his temperament weaknesses were slowness and laziness. When he read it himself, he freely admitted that he'd been "dragging his feet" on certain projects – not because he was busy enjoying life as I had presumed – but because he didn't want to put the effort in. We didn't even recognize his character weakness until we looked at his temperament.

Last, this book probably would never have been written had my firstborn and I not both been "Rabbits," each with our own personal "carrot patches" to administrate. I had to learn how to forgive my children for bouncing through my own carefully laid-out rows, then how to yield my rights to my patch to God, and finally how to count the "bouncers" (and other "Rabbits") as more important than the patch itself. Realizing that my choleric temperament has a tendency to "shoot for the goal" without considering potential pitfalls helped me to accept my daughter's need for detail and her (sometimes) good suggestions. And recognizing I also had strong Sanguine tendencies helped me to realize I was sometimes over-reacting to our Sanguine son because I was fearful when I saw him displaying the same hasty decisions I'd gotten in the habit of making.

Birth Order[36]

Speaking of first-borns, understanding the characteristics of birth order helps us to get a glimpse of life from each of our children's unique vantage points in the family. After getting the okay from Bill one gorgeous fall morning, I surprised the children at breakfast by announcing that we were leaving for the cabin – in fifteen minutes. Everyone cheered and scrambled to pack, except first-born Jonathan. Yes, the cabin *was* 500 miles away, but how was I to know that first-borns don't like spur-of-the-moment vacations? Or rashly-packed vans? Or unscheduled lifestyles? I thought he just needed to lighten up and I teased him for being a stick-in-the-mud. He did have a good time (once the shock wore off), but when I understood him better, I tried to give him the courtesy of a heads-up. That way, he could feel prepared and I still had the fun of surprising everyone else. **First-borns** tend to be conscientious, reliable achievers since they take their cues from adult role models (their parents) instead of another child "up the line."

It also surprised us to learn that **second-borns** are most influenced (for good or bad), not by parents, but by the first-born. That was encouraging to us as a sort of domino-effect began once we started regaining our first-born's heart. Knowing why second-borns were typically more competitive as well as gullible helped us to warn our second-born of certain traps.

We also learned that a **middle child** often feels left out or misunderstood. That helped us to troubleshoot real and potential problems with our own middle child. There are many variable dynamics, however, depending on gender and age gaps.

Learning Modality

While Jon and Kate (our first and third-born) were advancing academically at a fast clip, James (the second-born) was struggling to keep up. At age eleven his character was solid and he'd do anything we asked – if he was able. Staying at grade-level in academics, though, was one thing he wasn't able to do. He missed major points during silent reading (visual), and went blank or stressed out in oral drills in math or phonics (auditory).

But he could build with Legos for hours and jumped into any hands-on project he could find. It turned out that he had a **kinesthetic** learning modality.

Learning modality lets us know what type of learner our child is – visual, auditory or kinesthetic – which helps us to find the most effective study methods for that child. Being a kinesthetic (hands-on) learner didn't mean that he couldn't learn anything that was visual or auditory, but that he learned better kinesthetically. His dad, on the other hand, is an **auditory** learner and spent his college years sitting closed-eyed (and some teachers assumed sleeping) through classroom lectures so he could block out visual distractions. And Jonathan, a **visual** learner with an almost photographic memory, needed only to scan materials once to lock in major points. The rest of us seem to have more evenly balanced modalities.

Once we learned his modality we switched James' science and history to a computer-based curriculum hoping that the hands-on interaction of a keyboard would stimulate more learning. But it didn't, and he became one year older and one year further behind. He couldn't retain all his math facts or phonics sounds even though he drilled them, couldn't spell well, his handwriting was dreadful, and both he and I were near tears. He felt at a loss to learn, and I felt at a loss to find the key to his learning.

Right Brain/Left Brain Dominance

I finally became desperate enough to sincerely cry out to the Lord for him. Less than a week later, I "just happened to" turn to a radio broadcast in which the traits of the **right-brain dominant male**[37] were being discussed. Our son, it seemed, was a classic example – strong in music, art, or hands-on activities, but weak in spelling, handwriting or memorization. I learned that males who are right-brain dominant as children balance out after puberty, rapidly catching up on academics. I consumed books on the subject and suddenly we had a new understanding of our son.

I was concerned that if we pushed him too hard to get to grade level that he would burn out or lose any love of learning he may have left.[38] Since it was evident that his struggling academic performance wasn't a character flaw (he wasn't pretending not to understand or holding out on finishing lessons because he didn't want to do them), we tried something different. We stopped force-feeding math facts and spelling, subjects that were causing him to "choke," and decided to try letting him blossom academically on his own timetable. We had him fill his mornings with reading or listening to classics and Christian biographies or auto-biographies. After lunch, he was free to work on projects where he could learn practical hands-on skills.

> Since his character was strong, we tried something different.
>
> We stopped force-feeding, and let him blossom academically on his own timetable.

He thrilled to the change. What twelve year-old wouldn't enjoy crawling into a hammock with *The Adventures of Robinson Crusoe* or identifying with the struggles of men like William Carey, John Bunyan or George Mueller? We also gave him lots of classical music which he enjoyed. I tend to be a compartmental-type learner and I have a hard time concentrating if there is very much outside stimulus. I was surprised to see that James, along with Bill and several other children, could not only handle music going on while they studied or read, but thrived on it.

That year he logged over 100 hours learning to build, repair and maintain computers with his dad. He also spent two weeks with him helping him set up computer networks in offices around the state. Spending that much time one-in-one with his dad was a once-in-a-childhood experience that was an unforeseen benefit. Bill assigned several books on networking along with a term paper, which was his only written assignment that year. Bill then helped him to perfect the term paper for six weeks.

> We want to teach the child, not the curriculum.

The next year he took on more hands-on projects, one of them posting weekly messages to our support group's website.

I still had a concern that his ability might never catch up. But it did. He began to catch up around the age of fifteen, scoring "A"s on former material, and flying through subjects that had been so difficult for him before.

Once his academics began to catch up, however, we noticed that this same young man would regularly leave schoolwork unfinished to work on projects around the house. An un-requested repair on a VCR or a lawnmower could easily fill up his morning. I assumed that either he'd become accustomed to less bookwork and lacked the self-discipline to stay on track, or he was simply gravitating toward doing what he enjoyed over what was required. Then we read about the spiritual gifts listed in Romans 12.

Spiritual Gifts

As our children become older and begin to develop their Christian faith, understanding the characteristics of the spiritual gifts helps us to understand why they view themselves (the world, the church, their siblings and us) the way they do. It also helps us to help them transition into their particular place and mission in all of those worlds a little more smoothly.

Jamey's spiritual gift was **serving,** and we learned that a server sometimes places more importance on meeting other people's needs than their own. In other words, he really viewed the time he spent repairing something for us as more important than time spent on his own duties. It's interesting to note that this kinesthetic-learning son chose hands-on repair projects as his gift of serving, while his visual-learning brother volunteered for more visible needs, such as painting the house or picking up a cluttered room on a busy day.

Once we saw that our son was functioning from a motivation of truly serving, we were able to point out the dangers within his gift that could cause him to stumble, like leaving his own responsibilities unfulfilled. And because we understood his motivation, I no longer assumed he was simply trying to get out of an undesirable assignment. He learned why it was important to stay on task and we learned to accept him better.

In another situation, one of our teens was not telling us if any of his siblings misbehaved while he was babysitting. My initial response to him was disappointment in not being told the whole story. But when he told us he didn't have the heart to report them since they always asked forgiveness before we got home, I got it! His motivational gift of **mercy** was evident in many ways - and so was his need for instruction on how to be a firmer leader.

A person who has the motivational gift of **prophecy** will have a strong love of truth, but it's often displayed as criticism towards others whom they see as hypocritical. Life tends to be intense and black and white, with little room for mercy. We tried to help this child to learn the importance of mercy.

A young person with the gift of **encouragement** may need to learn discretion so he doesn't share too much information when trying to encourage someone else. A child with the gift of **teaching** may need to be taught how to conquer pride. Those with the gift of **organizing** might need to learn how to count people as more important than projects, and a **giver** may need to be learn to wait on God's direction rather than automatically jumping in to meet a need.

Emotional Immaturity

While physical and mental disabilities are easier to spot, emotional immaturity is much harder. Many times I've wondered, "Is this child's behavior due to lack of character or to lagging emotional development?" We came to the conclusion that a child is probably emotionally immature if he feels more comfortable playing with younger children than with his own age group, he acts foolishly (like the class clown) in any age group, he *wants* to please us but continues to behave immaturely, his offenses are not willfulness or rebellion but are more of the "forgetting" or irresponsible or childish-behavior type, and he's truly sorry for his offense (even though he does it again tomorrow). Daily life can be trying for the emotionally-immature child because he must still be governed by external consequences or motivated by external praise – consequences and praise in areas that a younger sibling no longer needs. It can also be difficult for his siblings who may expect more mature behavior from someone his age. How I

How I respond to the neediest child in his neediest ways on his neediest days sets the tone for everyone else's response to that child.

responded to the neediest child in his neediest ways on his neediest days set the tone for everyone else's response to that child.

Special needs[39]

Special Physical and Mental Needs

Parents whose children have mental or physical limitations know how trying it can be to face ongoing needs with no sign of relief. Those parents need more patience, understanding, acceptance, grace and love than they've ever needed before. They also need wisdom to know when attitudes or behavior need to be lovingly overlooked (and for how long), or when firm boundaries need to be lovingly enforced. Adult life will be even more difficult for a special needs child if he's been allowed to use his disability as an excuse for behavior that he could have controlled.

Parents whose children have been gifted with genius ability or great artistic, musical or athletic talent need wisdom to help their children discover the purpose for their gifts. They'll also want to keep a finger on the pulse of their children's mental, emotional and spiritual health. Extremely talented artists and composers, who are naturally more sensitive, can be more subject to depression. They can even feel like their gifts are burdensome or oppressive or that no one understands how they feel. And they'll also need wisdom to know when attitudes or behavior should be overlooked (and for how long), or when firm boundaries need to be enforced. Adult life for the exceptional child will also turn out to be difficult if he is used to letting his gifts serve as an excuse for wrong behavior.

How We Respond to Our Children's Unique Needs

How we respond to the most needy child in his most needy ways on his most needy days sets the tone for everyone else's response to that child. A child with limitations affects the whole family – for better or for worse. Parents and siblings tend to move in the direction of becoming more patient, more understanding and more loving, or they find themselves becoming more frustrated, more angry or more desensitized. Family members might even find themselves becoming more sensitive to those with the same disability outside the family, while becoming less patient at home. Like the fisherman who had to keep shifting so he didn't lose his catch, we have to ask the Lord to first shift and change *us*.

The term "special needs" usually refers to mental or physical disabilities. But our children *all* have special needs, and they are all unique.

If It Ain't Broke, Don't Fix It!

If you're facing a roadblock with your child and you're at a loss to figure out what it is, bring those concerns to the Lord and ask Him to guide you to the resources you'll need to help him. But remember that old adage: *If it ain't broke, don't fix it!* In other words, it's not necessary to learn about spiritual gifts if your children are very young, or learning modality and right-brain dominance if academics are easy, or special needs if there aren't any ongoing symptoms. We have enough to do already!

Conclusion

It's helpful to remember that whenever we're faced with situations beyond our understanding or control, we eventually discover our own limits. There is a dimension of God's love that we don't even experience until we come to the end of our own. I found some of my limits with our children, and because of those limits, discovered some of that Love. That's why I encourage parents to cry out to the Lord first for wisdom and to ask for His limitless love and grace. My natural self wants to think I'm competent and sophisticated and independent, but God wants us all to be child-like (in faith) and needy (of Him) and dependent (on His power).

Chapter Five: Commend Character

Good character is more to be praised than outstanding talent.
Most talents are, to some extent, a gift. Good character, by
contrast, is not given to us; we have to build it piece by piece,
by thought, by choice, courage and determination.
John Luther

I f getting to the root of a problem is like pulling weeds from a garden, commending character is like watering it.   Both are necessary for a healthy garden, but watering is much less work! It's also much more rewarding as our words soak into our children's hearts and we see them begin to develop their own good fruit.

I was reluctant to commend my children at first because I thought they would misinterpret my praise as approval for bad behavior. There were days, too, that I was at a loss to think of anything I could commend them for. Because people tend to see what they're looking for, an eye that's looking for fault will find fault, while one that's looking for good will find good. Even God, as good as He is allows Himself to be seen as twisted by people whose eye is bad.[40] At first I could only see weeds. I wanted it to produce beautiful fruit, so I felt my time would be better spent weeding the massive overgrowth rather than taking the time to water and fertilize a tiny bud here or there.

I'd also seen mothers who overdid it, who praised their children with a saccharine-smile or in a pseudo-cheery, condescending manner for every little thing. Their children didn't have a higher standard to live up to. Their mother's praise condescended down to the children's comfortable, fleshly standard of living, and the children learned to camp in that pleasant, evidently praiseworthy place. Pleasant, that is, until Mother realized they didn't want to break camp!

I will admit here that I have praised a child for doing *nothing* – when the nothing was the absence of the usual misbehavior. My hope was to "prime the pump" and stimulate a hunger for more praise. I also must admit that, while doing this a little can help move a child out of a rut of wrong behavior, doing it too much can cause him to settle in for more. On the one hand, we relate to our children on their level, and try to show them, baby-step by baby-step how to grow. But if we camp with them for too long on a level below their ability, we can find ourselves abandoning the standards for fear of losing the child. Then we're both lost! Our children need us to hang in there with them, yet draw them over, away from living for self, to living for the Lord. That type of character growth doesn't come naturally – it goes against their nature and against ours. Sometimes a little extra praise can really help. Too much, though, for too little effort, or offered insincerely, can promote complacency (and even contempt).

> We want them to learn how to give expecting nothing in return.

Real affirmation is just encouraging them while it's called, Today.[41] It's giving warm, natural attention for right living in a natural way. Fred. Rogers from Mr. Rogers' Neighborhood actually became my model for natural, warm, respectful conversation with a child. We just talk to our child in a natural way that lets him know he's on the right track and we're glad of it. It might mean we offer that enthusiastic praise to a preschooler, or give a quick hug to a ten year-old with a quiet, "Well done," or give a knowing smile and word of praise to a teen. It just needs to be a genuine word from us, and connect with that child in a way he can receive it. We want to make sure he knows how proud of him we are that he made a good decision.

If we overdo it, or if it's not the real thing, it can backfire. I'll admit that both Bill and I have fainted on cue (in mock shock of character growth) to make a child laugh. It was a fun way to drive home a point.

I knew if I were to have any hope of breaking the cycle of misbehavior and correction in which we seemed hopelessly stuck, that I'd have to begin commending the tiny buds of good character (obedience, patience, faithfulness, love, sound decisions, etc.) that were already blossoming.

> I had to learn how to regularly, gently, casually, sprinkle drops of conversational praise for little things.

I had to try to strike a balance somewhere in the middle and learn how to regularly, gently, casually, sprinkle drops of conversational praise for little things.

"Say, I saw your little brother with your beloved baseball glove this morning. Did you loan it to him?"

"Yes, I told him he could use it."

"That is way kind, Kiddo. You're the best. (Casual squeeze, kiss or smile.)"

I say "commend them in a casual way" because I noticed that relaxed, unfussy, matter-of-fact affirmation created an atmosphere that said in unspoken words, "I know you're going to be someone who makes the right decisions (goes the extra mile/hangs in there to let patience have its perfect work, etc.) and I just want you to know that I noticed (that I thought what you did was wonderful, that you were an encouragement to me, that I'm so proud of you, that you're just okay with me)."

As soon as a child succeeds in a new course or attitude, even in a very small way, we want to mention that we noticed.

One of Bill's standards for our home is that each one's personal property is supposed to be protected, especially from younger, less-trained siblings. But I sometimes let that standard slip. Then I had weeds of resentment toward younger siblings because of unchecked abuse of personal property. Other times I'd go to the younger sibling and let him know great I thought it was that his brother loaned him something that meant so much to him, and that I'd be so impressed if he returned it when he said he would to the place his brother wanted. I'd have to make a note in my planner to casually mention to him later that I noticed and appreciated his faithfulness, or I would forget!

"Say, good job on getting your brother's toy back when you said you would. You just keep growing in faithfulness these days, don't you?" (Small kiss.)

We might wait until bedtime and snuggle up to a young child that rarely remembers to get his morning chores done and say, "Do you know what would be great? It would be so wonderful if you feed the dog before breakfast tomorrow, just like your chart says. That would be so amazing!" We don't expect rapid growth just because we begin praising them. We wouldn't start out by saying, "You would please me so much if you pick up your room before dinner tomorrow, and remember to feed the dog each day without being asked, and if you see something that needs to be done, you just do it!" That sounds more like, "You would please me so much – *if you were just someone else!*"

Once we see our children respond we try to praise them quickly and genuinely.

"Say, that was great when you didn't follow your friends running through the museum halls this afternoon. And you didn't get an attitude when they ran off. And you held the door open for others, even though it meant that you didn't get the best seat for the program. I just want to remind you that God sees and He'll you for every small thing you do for Him. And I'm really proud of the kinds of decisions you're making lately!"

Commending them for character helps them grow in character. If we praise them for their accomplishments, they can get the idea that we're measuring them by accomplishments. If we tend to be performance-oriented, then to learn to commend character, we have to see the character behind the performance – the effort that makes the performance what it's. Character is found in the effort-to-ability ratio, and it's that character – that effort behind the performance – that we want to let them know is most important. We have to think in terms of what kind of person my child is becoming, not what kind of things my child will accomplish.

For example, if we see that our child practices an instrument faithfully, but we only tell him what a wonderful musician he's becoming or how much we enjoy his music, he may only connect our praise with his performance. We can still tell him how much we enjoy his music, but we can add that we're proud of the diligence we see during practice, or the thoughtfulness to put practice off during the baby's nap, or faithfulness when he remembered to finish up after the baby woke up.

We give messages of praise in hundreds of ways over hundreds of days of what is truly important to us. If we display the "A" paper because it's an "A", or call grandparents excitedly about the trophy, ribbon or award, or center our celebrations around the win, the performance or the prize – we're praising performance over character. But if a child sees that we display the project that was most improved (especially if it only looks like a "C" compared to the "A" paper that didn't require the same effort to produce), if he overhears us telling grandparents how pleased we are because of his winning attitude (whether he won anything or not), if we celebrate milestones in decisions rather than receiving of awards, then we're letting him know that his character is more important than his performance. We're telling him that who he *is* is more important than what he does. We have to really want our children to succeed in character before we want them to succeed in the world. We need to assure them that God values traits such as responsibility, honesty, dependability and loyalty even if future bosses or colleagues don't. And that God will reward. This is preparing them for real life.

It helps to take a moment to fast-forward ten or twenty years to gain perspective. How do we envision our child as an adult? If what he does matters more (or even as much) to us than who he becomes, then we will inadvertently praise him for what he does – no matter how much we try to praise him for character.

> The person who shapes the character of a child affects everyone in that adult child's world.

If we've swung too far in the opposite direction, and view the world as "against" him and we envision his adulthood as a time when everything will somehow be resolved for him – then we'll fall into praising him only for his strengths, or for traits that revolve around his personal happiness.

If, on the other hand, we tend to be child-oriented (our child's happiness, decisions, or will are the center of our focus), then to learn how to praise character, we have to see that he will never be a happy, balanced adult without good character.

We don't want to get into the habit of praising them for character *deficiencies* either by making light of them, or warmly teasing about them, "My, your ears work well when I'm speaking privately to your brother!" It wouldn't be surprising, then, to see more eaves-dropping become a cute way of trying to get more attention. I don't think there's anything wrong with diffusing correction with occasional teasing. I certainly do my share of teasing in our home (and have earned a little payback from our adult children and teens). But if our default-mode for correcting them is light-hearted attention for misbehavior, it won't be long before misbehavior is the norm. They want our attention and they'll do what works to get it. We let our children know what's really important to us, how they please us, by our warm, genuine, positive attention.

We've seen some pretty amazing instances of the Lord turning one of our hearts around overnight, but most of the time growth is slow and we're supposed to be patient with each other. We wouldn't expect a five year-old who was accustomed to getting his own way to suddenly *want* to go to bed on time, any more than we'd expect a twelve year-old who had a habit of procrastinating to suddenly get all his assignments in on time – just because we started commending him. It's more reasonable to expect him to begin to respond in small ways.

It's rewarding to see how encouraging our children changes them. What's really amazing is to see how it changes us! I don't know what happened first when I began to commend them more, whether it was my eyes that started to open to character qualities I'd been blind to, or whether my praise caused a burst of growth that made it possible for me to finally see little blooms over the weeds. The difference was definitely noticeable. There was a marked relationship between more sincere nurturing and praise, and less need for correction, when I punctuated busy days with encouragement.

"By the way, I knew you were as hungry as I was in the van when we got home so late from all those errands. I don't know about you, but I was feeling like I was really on the edge. But, when I looked in the rear-view mirror and saw you reading to your brother, well – that really encouraged me. You ended up being an example to me. Thanks! You're just the best, Sweetheart."

If we don't see much progress, we can make our encouragement a little more tangible. For a child who's prone to laziness we can grade math assignments with points given for neatness, or for double-checking problems instead of for correct answers. As he is genuinely praised and tangibly rewarded for neatness and accuracy, correct answers will usually begin to come naturally, and laziness will be recognized as more costly than neatness, since he has to go back and complete the lesson again (and again) if it's not neat.

Rewarding a child with praise and more liberty is best, but giving tangible rewards can be okay, too. We just want to be careful giving money, candy or other pleasures, since it can set them up to for selfish motivations for doing good. We want them to build gradual strength doing what's right because it's right, and because it pleases God, not for material gain. They can still earn money or treats for a job well done, of course, and enjoy some of life's pleasures, like candy bars, from time to time. Parents today just tend to reward children too much for too little, so we now have a generation of children who haven't experienced delayed gratification. We want to be careful with what we use to motivate them. To motivate by Scriptures tenderly shared, by love, by praise and by a oneness of fellowship is a most effective way. Sometimes, they, being immature and weak, might need a little extra stimulus. A little tangible reward can be good, but too much reward, or constant pleasure-centered rewards, can cause our children to stumble.

If a child isn't responding to encouragement or tangible rewards, we need to bring outward pressure. If he still hurries through assignments that need more attention, if it still takes him all day to do what he has the capability to complete in an hour, if he still misses deadlines that he's able to meet, then he needs to have the "freedom" of using his own playtime or free time to finish the project. That's a reasonable consequence that he must pay. An unreasonable consequence is for us to bear the cost by helping, nagging or reacting. We want to allow him to stand or to fall within safe boundaries of clear expectations and consequences. Weekly accountability (or daily, or even moment-by-moment depending on maturity), with clearly understood consequences is important. This is bringing in outward pressure when encouragement fails. If we haven't won our child's, though, or if there is unforgiveness or unresolved hurts from past issues, our praise will probably fall on deaf ears.

If outward pressure begins to produce results, we then want to praise him for his willingness to comply, even if we believe he'd revert back to his old ways if the pressure were removed. We want to "prime the pump," helping him get used to being commended for doing what's right. When he's had some practice being faithful, the outward pressure can slowly be removed. Our tendency will be to remove pressure at the first glimpse of growth. But, growth rarely happens in a slow, steady climb. It's usually two steps forward, one step back. We have to be patient.

Children take their first cues about who they are from the people with whom they spend the most time. If we have a secret fear they aren't going to turn out well, we'll project that fear to them, since the mouth speaks out of that which fills the heart.42 Secret fears rise to the surface in moments of crisis, and people tend to believe what's conveyed in the heat of the moment (So, that's what you really believe about me!). That's why it's so important for a mom to pour out her fears to the Lord and ask Him deliver her from them. We don't want to pass our fears on to them.

Young people sometimes act out because they're drowning in the waters of self-rejection, and their flailing at everyone in sight is their effort to find air. They really want to believe they can learn to swim, but if the people around them are telling them they're going to drown, they can't help but lose hope. If they have someone in their life who believes they're not only going to survive, but that they're going to be a really great swimmer despite those waters, that belief can be their raft back to safety. Everyone needs encouragement, reassurance and commendation. It's one of the ways we fulfill Jesus' command to love one another.

Each one of us influences someone else by the attention we give them in regard to the things that really matter to us. Parents are in a unique position of influence through positive affirmation and attention. Praise stimulates growth. When we commend our children for their character, it serves as a buffer to correction, and as emotional support for tough decisions. It's also a powerful tool that helps keep disappointments in perspective, and discouragement at bay. What we encourage our children in now will influence their direction as adults. The saying, "The hand that rocks the cradle rules the world" could be restated, "The person who shapes the character of a child affects everyone in that adult child's world."

Chapter Six: Cut the Ties

Take your son, your only son...Genesis 22:2

Ties of Personal Needs...

By the time our oldest was about twelve, we were making steady progress in regaining his heart, while I was building a little more consistent character in to mine. However, there were still times when he seemed to overreact to me. His attitude then caused the scientifically-proven equal-and-opposite, knee-jerk reaction in me. He pushed my "hot buttons." I'd find myself hitting a 10 on the Momzilla Meter, instantly issuing consequences, or trying to perform "heart surgery" on him with a sharp tongue as the cutting instrument. Needless to say, it was easy to get discouraged with both of our failures during those times, and to forget that we'd ever made any progress at all.

One morning one of our sons was particularly critical towards his siblings. I faithfully took him each time to determine the cause, to try to help him to resolve it. Each time we talked, he took responsibility for his actions, and accepted the consequences. But inside he seemed resistant and distant. By the end of the day, he was as irritable as ever and I was showing signs of wear. His last remark prompted me to appear instantly on the scene, in a sort of Super-Mom fashion (leaping over small children in a single bound). And there we stood, mother and son, eye to eye, toe to toe, will to will. I think my eyes may have been bulging. I know the eyes of the child I leapt over were.

The details are fuzzy at this point, but after giving him some type of lecture, he looked up at his mother with the bulging eyes and said coolly, "Mom? Do you realize that you're overreacting?"

Buzz. It was the sound of the Momzilla Meter hitting 10. *Me, overreacting? Me,* who had poured out my soul to him all morning, trying to help him with *his* problems? *Me,* who had given up so much to love him, train him, teach him – who was only asking that he be kind to those around him? *Overreacting?   Well,   this   pint-sized,   self-proclaimed psychologist hadn't seen overreacting yet!*

I sent him to his room, and I went to mine. I closed the door. Loudly, if I remember. I was discouraged, I was angry, and I was sad. I also felt very needy, and I cried out to the Lord for help.

Lord, I don't know what to do with my son! Please help!

As I stood there sulking and half-praying, a picture I'd seen years before of Abraham offering Isaac came to mind. I thought about that scene for a long moment. It certainly didn't seem very inspirational – scene of parent-standing-over-teen-with-sharp-knife-in-hand   –   especially considering the dark emotions I was feeling.

I decided I should probably put my son on the altar, too. *Perhaps*, I reasoned, *that was why that picture came to mind when I cried out to the Lord.*

> I realized that what I thought were good *desires* were actually *needs*. And it was those needs that triggered my quick response to his misbehavior.

When I tried to imagine putting my son on the altar, I felt a tug of ties in my heart attached to my son that I had never seen before. Before that moment, I thought that all my *desires* for my son (that his character wouldn't fail, that he would please the Lord) were unselfish. In that moment, I realized that they were really my own *needs*. My needs that had triggered my quick response to his every misbehavior that morning.

One need was for my son to respect me. When he acted disrespectfully I corrected him in knee-jerk fashion. It was enlightening, and yet painful, to see. I lifted an imaginary knife and brought it down, asking the Lord to cut my personal need to be respected by my son from between us. I didn't know that my need had kept me from teaching him how to give respect. I only knew then that it had kept me from getting him completely on that altar. It was a wonderful experience. I felt freer inside knowing that something was gone that had silently pulled at me for so long.

But that thrill lasted only a moment as I tried to put him back on the altar, only to discover another need. This time I saw that my reputation was tied to his behavior. Ouch! How could that possibly be and I never saw it? And then a sinking feeling that I had known it all along, but had never faced it. I realized his lack of character would reflect on me, and that I *needed* him to behave to protect my reputation. Again I raised that imaginary knife and asked the Lord to help me to cut my need for my son to make right decisions (not knowing that it would later free me to teach him how to make right decisions). Just then a verse from Job came to mind.

Though He slay me, yet will I trust in Him.[43]

I wondered what that verse could mean just then. I didn't think it would be hard for me to trust in God even if I knew He was going to slay me. And then I remembered that invisible knife.

Oh, no! If I really gave my son to the Lord, and He allowed <u>him</u> to be slain before the ripe old age I <u>needed</u> him to live to, would I still trust in Him?

That was very hard. I asked the Lord to please give me the strength to cut away at this need, and the faith to trust Him with my son for whatever end He would allow.

Again, relief. And again, another troubling thought.

Dying physically is one thing. But, what if I surrendered my son to the Lord, and He allowed him to die spiritually?

Another verse.

He who loves father or mother more than Me is not worthy of Me; and he who loves son or daughter more than Me is not worthy of Me. Matthew 10:37

I knew I was at a crossroads of being asked whether I loved father, mother, son or daughter more than the Lord. Cutting away at this last need was like a slaying, indeed.

Though He slay me, yet will I trust in Him. Job 13:15

One by one, I was able to see personal needs that were directly connected to my son's behavior. And one by one the Lord helped me to cut them. I could immediately tell they were cut because I could immediately see my son in a new light. I could see *his* needs instead of mine. The Momzilla Meter was at zero. Compassionate understanding had taken its place.

That's not to say it remained at zero from that day on. But, I did start to become a little more nurturing. My thoughts began to change from, "Oh, no, he's doing that again!" to, "Lord, what do You want me to do to help him so he doesn't fall so much?" Instead of reacting to *my* need for him to be more respectful, I could see *his* need to learn respect. Instead of my need to have a child who didn't say hurtful or embarrassing things, I was able to be a little more humble and try to think about why he might be acting that way, rather than what others would be thinking about me. I began had much less personal and emotional stake in his success or failure. I felt much less discouraged or threatened when he did wrong. My hot buttons were less push-able, overreaction to his behavior diminished, and the dynamics in our relationship and our home brightened. When I considered his misbehavior, I identified with him more, understanding that we were in the same mess, in need of the same Deliverer.

We need to make sure our personal worth and emotional needs are separated from our children's behavior. A child senses the strain of parental needs tied to his behavior, performance or decisions. He feels it whenever his departure from his parents' expectations triggers strong, negative reactions. If he tries to make the cut himself, his efforts to get free can slash deep into his parents' hearts. This severing of needs lays a fresh beginning for loving acceptance of our children – whether they fulfill our *desires* for them, or not.

It's possible to become so consumed with the gift, that we neglect or forget the Giver. The very thing that I wanted, I had to be willing to lose. The one I was willing to die *for*, I had to be willing to die *to*. God's wonderful, mysterious Kingdom, so full of paradoxes to our natural minds, requires that we die in order to live, give in order to receive, and turn away from our needs to see them fulfilled. I gained my son back that day only after I died to everything I needed him to be.

My character is who I am apart from my child's successes or failures.

We dedicated all our children to the Lord when they were born, but I wonder now how we could have ever realized what we were doing at the time. There is a world of difference between dedicating a baby to God, and surrendering *ourselves* to God in the midst of each parenting challenge. True dedication is only possible when our children fail us, fail themselves, or fail God – or when we fail them, fail ourselves, or fail God.

> Jesus had no tolerance for people who said they spoke for His Father, but laid burdens on men's shoulders that were hard to bear.

If we use our own emotional reactions to our children as a signal (whether they're overreactions or underreactions), we can call on the Lord to show us what needs to be placed on the altar, and which ties need to be cut. It's the difference between *needing* our children to have strong character and *earnestly desiring* them to.

Ties of Judgment
~because of Similar Weaknesses or Sins

Only a year after cutting those ties I found myself getting more and more irritated by another one of our children. As long as things around him went smoothly, he could run smoothly. But he got angered by the smallest difficulties and pulled off-course by the smallest distractions.

He responded well to my praise, but only as long as he never left my sight. His need to be continually reinforced was costing me mounds of time, energy and patience. Whenever we talked to him he was always sorry, truly sincere, had the deepest love, and was full of good intentions. But, once those good intentions had to be attached to follow-through or personal cost, he floundered. He reminded me of the son in Matthew 21 who said to his father, "I will!" but never did. Had we enforced all his consequences for all the rules that he consistently forgot, he would have been on KP until he was twenty-one. I finally realized that he was emotionally immature. I began to fear that he would never mature.

One day, frustrated over his last childish act, I exploded. "Must you *always* insist on having things *your* way?!" Then I suddenly had the uncomfortable feeling I was looking into a mirror. And I wondered if God might want to ask me the very same question.

Only a few years before, Bill and I decided to try to become debt-free. We sold our contemporary 3/2 in the suburbs and bought an old, wood-frame, tin-roofed house in the county that had been built in 1883. We had four children at the time and my father was living with us. True, the house had no heat, no air-conditioning, no fences, no closets, no cabinets and only one bathroom. But, we decided we could add those things in time. More importantly, we had reduced our debt significantly.

I was full of excitement about moving our family from a busy subdivision and small yard to a place with tall ceilings, more square footage, more yard, and a more pioneer-type, homey, atmosphere that felt similar to that of, well, *Little House on the Prairie*.

Carolyn Ingalls was a wonderful wife and mother, and she survived without heat or air-conditioning in a one-room cabin,

I reasoned. *And in freezing Minnesota. Surely I can survive in Florida without a few conveniences.*

And I did survive. Very well.

Until Day Three. On Day Three I got hot. And real sweat (not romantic, nostalgic, historical sweat) began pouring down my real face (not rugged-yet-smiling, pioneer-type face) as I lugged cookware and plates back and forth between bedroom and kitchen (no kitchen cabinets to store them in yet), with a toddler wrapped around one ankle, and preschoolers pulling everything else off of makeshift, doorless shelves in the kitchen. The heat index was 110°. Inside.

Bill arrived home that night in his air-conditioned car having driven from his air-conditioned office. I told him I'd had a revelation.

"Honey, it turns out I'm not Caroline Ingalls from *Little House on the Prairie* after all."

He looked up at me.

"I think I'm really Zsa Zsa Gabor from *Green Acres*."

"It was Eva."

"Huh?"

"*Eva* Gabor starred in *Green Acres*, not Zsa Zsa."[44]

"Okay, then, I'm *Eva* Gabor."

This time he peered at me dryly over his glasses. I suddenly remembered what a bombshell Eva Gabor was. I had the feeling he wasn't getting my point.

"Okay, fine! I'm not Eva Gabor, either," I cried. "But this *is* Green Acres, *and I 'vant to go back to 'za city!*"

Bill patiently told me that if God provided the money for us to get a different house, we would definitely move. But, he just didn't think we were supposed to go further into debt.

Still I cried out to him to please take me back to civilization, back to our old "Egypt" where life was easier (and cooler) in the bondage of higher debt.

Six months later winter one of the worst cold snaps in history arrived. I wasn't hot anymore. I was frozen. And I begged Bill for a woosher.

"A what?" he asked.

"A woosher. You know. That little dial on the wall that I used to saunter over to at my leisure and turn with my pinkie finger to hear – *whoosh!* Instant heat!"

I was now expecting Child Number Six and knew there was no money in the budget for central heat. We had a wood stove, but I dreaded waking up to the now 45° kitchen and waiting two hours for the rest of the house to warm up. I wasn't happy.

When crying out to Bill didn't work, I resorted to crying out to God.

Lord, please, please, please deliver me from this house!

I cried out to God for several years, but no deliverance came. So I tried to deliver myself. I looked for other houses. I tried to figure out a way to handle a part-time job and still be home with the children. I put pressure on Bill to take on a bigger mortgage. But, I couldn't deliver myself. And, still, I wasn't happy.

That was where I was that morning, listening to my own words echo back at me through the mirror of my son's life. Was I going to insist on having this my own way?

I realized that morning that I had been angry with God about the difficulties that I'd had to endure for the past couple of years (dismissing the fact that the house had been my find). When life with its conveniences had gone fairly smoothly, I ran fairly smoothly. But in this house, I'd been getting easily angered by the smallest difficulties, and got pulled off-course from the goals we'd set. Whenever I talked to the Lord about it, I was always sorry, truly sincere, had the deepest love, and was full of good intentions. But when those good intentions had to be hitched to follow-through or personal cost, I floundered. I felt like the son in Matthew 21 who said to his father, "I will!" but never did. Had God enforced all my earned consequences from all the good intentions and promises I'd broken, I should have been assigned to live in that house until I was 121!

It had been frustrating enough to know I had been overreacting to my son and to not know why. It felt even worse to know I was reacting to the same sins and problems I had in my own life. Just knowing seemed to discourage to me.

If I haven't overcome in this area after all these years, I glowered, *how can I expect this child to overcome? And how can I train him if I'm not trained?*

A child's bad behavior does require us to set tighter boundaries, or to suspend privileges. But those restrictions only keep him from acting out his sin. They don't teach him how to overcome it.

We have to receive deliverance from our own sins to be able to show our children the way. Otherwise, we can only point and say, "Go to the Lord. He will help." A better way is to say, "Follow me, and let me help show you the way. Follow me as I follow the Lord."[45]

> A better way is to say, "Follow me, and let me help show you the way. Follow me as I follow the Lord."

If we're overreacting to a child, or making stricter rules or consequences than are reasonable, we should look in our own life to see if we have the same type of problem. I had been guilty of the same sins of ungratefulness and shallow commitment that had been getting on my nerves when I saw them in my son. When I saw that, my prayers began to change.

Lord, please, please, please deliver me! Not from this house – but from myself!

Ties of Fear

There are also times that we might *underreact* to our child's obvious problems by refusing to recognize them, by calling them something other than sin, by hoping that it's just a stage that he'll grow out of, by resigning ourselves to it, or by not making him accountable for his behavior.

Some parents are even afraid of their own children. They might be afraid of his failures (*What if I don't know how to help him?*), or afraid of their failures (*What if I pass my problems on to him?*), or afraid of his needs (*What if we can't meet them?*), or afraid to bring correction (*What if he suffers, or becomes angry, or doesn't like me, or rejects me?*).

Parents who aren't able to let a child to suffer appropriate consequences usually have strong emotional needs (or ties), either to their child, or to a philosophy that conflicts with Scripture. They usually end up in power struggles with their children, and the children often win. If we don't bring correction (which is not the same as the *condemning* judgment), then our child runs the risk of incurring God's judgment when he's older.

Ties of Delight: Making Idols out of Our Children

God says He is a jealous God, and that He wants us to love Him first and best. Anything that sneaks into our hearts and takes His special place becomes an idol. Children can be very good at sneaking their way into the center, especially when we first meet them! I realized that when I held our firstborn for the first time. I really and truly loved Bill, but when I saw our son I knew I would lay down my life for him. Being that dear to us makes it an easy slide center

Our children belong right next to God's place in our hearts. We moms need to keep an eye on our hearts to make sure those cute little things aren't snuggling themselves down for the long haul in God's rightful place.

Conclusion

There's something about being a parent, something about loving someone more than we love ourselves, that motivates us to change. Some things go on the altar before we have children. But some things we don't even recognize until we see them reproduced in a child like a little mirror reflecting back at us. We don't want to see our problems repeated in our children's lives. If we do, we can ask the Lord for deliverance. As we are set free we, can better help our children to be set free.

Chapter Seven: When Our Children Fail
Accepting Failures, Disappointments and Trials

*If I take care of my character, my reputation will
take care of itself. Dwight L. Moody*

When Our Children Fail

There are several important things we should do when our children fail.

Accept Our Child

The first is to accept our child, exactly as he is, while he's still in his failures and weaknesses, and as though he will never be free of them. This feels so very hard, and seems to go against what we are working for. But it is what love does.

We still set boundaries and issue consequences, listen compassionately and continue to invest in him. But without high emotional taxation – *because we don't need that child to change.* And we have to be willing to keep doing so. It doesn't mean we embrace the sin, or excuse the behavior which can stem from that sin. Grieving for a child's poor decisions is not the same as withholding affection because he remains in his failure. Accepting our child means we don't cut him off if he doesn't change.

> Everyone needs to know that someone in this world loves them whether they make the standard or not.

This is our test of love! Every single person needs to know that someone in this world loves them whether they make the standard or not. If they don't find that "someone" at home, they'll look for someone else who will accept them.

Children can sense our motivation (*our need* that they change) before we even recognize it ourselves. Unless we accept them as they are (he might always be lazy, she may always be critical, he may always have that learning disability or may never mature), we aren't really accepting *them*, but merely attempting to change or train them. Even though that changing and training may be for their own good, we will make little headway without unconditional love.

This is actually God's love shining through us. God loves and accepts us exactly as we are, *before* He asks us to change. While we were yet in sin, Christ died for us. It's the security of that acceptance that makes the idea of change feel so safe, and even desirable.

Placing our child unchanged on the altar of our hearts is a costly sacrifice for a parent. We're not really giving *him* to God; we're surrendering our dreams and hopes for him, and dying to the right to change him. That's the only way he'll feel safe enough to want to change.

Cry out to the Lord

Second, I have to sincerely cry out to the Lord for that child. When we sincerely pray for that child, I sometimes see things in myself that He wants to change. Other times we might think of something we're supposed to say to that child, or do for him. Sometimes a friend or a relative or even a stranger tells us something we need to hear, or our research yields a resource that gives help.

I "happened" to turn on a radio broadcast on the way to the airport one day when the learning traits of the right-brain dominant male were being discussed. It was only a few days after I began sincerely calling on the Lord for help for my son. That broadcast had the help he needed at that very time of his life, and yet I had never heard of the effects of right-brain dominance before that day.

It's tempting to think we're supposed to pray for our children but not accept them as they are. Accepting them is where *we* are changed. It's one of those places we learn to shift so we don't lose the catch.

To come to a place where we can love those whom God has given to us to love without requiring that they change first is Love Divine! To be free enough to be warm and gracious to a child in the middle of his mess, while still enforcing necessary boundaries and consequences, gives him a secure environment in which he can risk future change. It gives our love credibility. It's giving God permission to change us even if our child is never changed. It's what makes our prayers for him more genuine.

> Character is who we are when we don't get what we want.
> It's who we are when we don't get what we think we deserve.

It's natural for us to want our children to have stronger character than we do. But it's not possible to teach that which we do not know, or to require that which we haven't lived. To *effect* change, we have to be willing to *be* changed. Depending on our personal experiences, it may take deep change. Teaching our children to accept disappointments, their trials and themselves as a foundation of strong character may take personal change of the deepest kind.

Handling Disappointments

Every truly great leader has learned how to accept failure and disappointment. We want them to know how to lose graciously, how to face trials and how to accept failures. It's in this context that we can actually count our disappointments as "all joy"[46] – because we believe it has a higher meaning.

If we want to teach our children how to graciously handle the disappointments in life, it really helps if they can see us graciously handle the disappointments in life. Our children will pick up on our outlook and attitudes and will learn to respond as we do.

I missed this lesson when our children competed in extra-curricular events many years ago. My Momzilla Meter pegged out over unfair results. It never occurred to me to tell our children that unfair things happen, or that they could use them as means to a more important lesson. The only lesson I could see was how the problem should be fixed for the next time. It's not a bad thing to try to correct something that's unfair, but my motivation was wrong. Consequently, our child missed the wonderful lesson God had planned for him through those circumstances. How sensible to allow our children to gain experience in facing situations that seem unfair before they leave our home. They'll certainly experience them again and again as adults.

> We learn more about *ourselves* by losing than what we would have learned by winning.

We don't want to teach our children how to win or how to be successful. We want to teach them how to do their best and how to have faith for God's best, even when they come up short on man's scale. Our children need to know that sometimes they'll lose. They also need the experience of losing. Woe unto us if we only let them do what they're good at, and woe unto our children if they succeed at everything they try. It's good for everyone to do their best and come in second, or even last. A better experience yet – to believe we should have won, and to lose still! That's because what we learn about *ourselves* by losing or suffering injustice is far more valuable than what we would have gained by winning. Character is who we are when we don't get what we want. It's who we are when we don't get what we think we deserve.

Accepting Trials

Even when God wants to deliver us from trials, we have to first accept the trials to be set free from them. While I was living in our old "Green Acres" house I complained regularly within the hearing of our children. One day I stopped "crying out to Bill" and began crying out to the Lord to deliver us.

The day after my first sincere prayer, ceramic tiles began falling off the shower wall. I cried out to the Lord again and the roof sprung four new leaks. I prayed again and a hole appeared on the porch floor. After more prayers for help drywall started peeling, doorknobs fell off, the septic tank backed up and the shed began to leak. While Bill was spending every spare moment making repairs, I was emptying his wallet at the home improvement store. I felt a bit like George Bailey in *It's a Wonderful Life* when he received a "sock in the jaw" right after his prayer for help in the bar. How could I accept these trials? How could I ever count them as "all joy?" It felt impossible to accept living there and ridiculous to look for good to come out of it. I became discouraged again and my negative attitude spread to everyone in the house.

One afternoon while making dinner, I was pondering my sorry state of affairs when I picture popped into my mind. It was a speeding football repeatedly spiraling towards me. I somehow knew that the ball represented all the trials of our old house. Okay, yes, I'm a mommy and I think in pictures.

It seemed like the first few times God allowed the ball to be tossed, I had quickly ducked to get out of the way. With more tosses I could see myself turning away, denying that the ball was even being thrown – and then bracing as it actually hit me. *This is ridiculous,* I thought as I stirred spaghetti sauce. But, more thoughts came.

Another toss. This time I could see myself retire to the sidelines, cross my arms over my chest and refuse to play.

Nothing I did could make that ball go away – not denying it, not bracing for it, not rejecting it and not giving up and pouting about it. That ball, full of the trials I wished I could escape, just kept coming.

Then I had the idea that the next time it was tossed, I should open up my arms and catch it. I wondered what would happen if I did. What about all these inconveniences and frustrations? Was I supposed to just open my arms and accept them? That would really hurt. I might get bruised or I might fall. But I didn't sense that the Coach was interested in giving me a different position.

As I finished making dinner, I stretched out the arms of my heart, so to speak, and braced myself to receive that ball, the symbol of the house with all its trials. I accepted that fact that we'd probability never move, that I might always be hot in the summer and cold in the winter, that we might never have a second bathroom, that repairs would have to wait until all the children were through braces and school and cars and college, that I would never be able to entertain friends or family in hot weather and that I might never be able to live in a house that I liked.

Whack! It *did* hurt to accept that! The impact of it hit me right in my tastes, hopes, dreams, plans, wants, comfort and pride. And I staggered. For a few weeks I felt like wearing black as I mourned the death of all my escape-plans. But I didn't fall. When I caught my balance, I felt stronger. I'd used muscles I didn't even know I had. And I was freer. It was because I was putting my flesh to death.

Our children will naturally be unsure about accepting difficult situations. Our example will help them. An important part of "Character 101" is the "lab." Students need a certain amount of trust that the "character experiments" will work. It helps to know that the teacher has been through the lesson before.

Helping Our Children to Accept Themselves

Character is what you are in the dark. Dwight L. Moody

If our child has a low self-esteem, it means he can't accept God's love *(I'm not worth it),* or that he can only accept His love with conditions *(I must be a better person, choose a higher standard, do a better job).* If we can accept him with his failures (accept that he's weak in an area, might always be weak), it will help him to accept himself (admit he's weak in an area, perhaps may always be weak).

If we've struggled to accept ourselves, our child may also struggle to accept himself. We want to help him understand that if he remains in denial about failures or runs from them that he'll put unrealistic expectations on himself, and consequently on those around him. Accepting himself as he is will give him a more compassionate heart. A person's perception of God changes once he accepts his own failures. God becomes bigger, His mercy greater, His love deeper. If we can help him understand that God loves him as he is *(We love Him because He first loved us)*, he'll be free to choose what's best for his soul – love for God and others. Failure can be a great teacher once we accept it. Acceptance doesn't breed complacency, but gratefulness.

Chapter Eight: Teach Them to Live for a Higher Purpose than Themselves

But he that is <u>greatest</u> among you will be your servant.
Matthew 23:11

"**I** don't want to raise *good* kids. I want to raise *great* kids!"

I heard myself blurt these words out to my mother-in-law and her mother as they laid a newly-finished quilt across a bed for me to admire.

Don't ask me why, having never taken a parenting class, and while my firstborn was still in diapers, I felt the urge to announce to my in-laws that what anyone else would have been happy with wasn't good enough for me. Looking back to that day in 1982, I think I wanted to assure those women that I did have hopes of one day being good at something domestic.

Bill and I had spent the weekend with his large, Southern family, and everyone had just finished a hearty Southern meal of tender, perfectly-seasoned roast with rich, brown gravy, hand-picked lima beans, home-grown slices of tomatoes and peppers, and fluffy home-made biscuits covered in home-made cane syrup.

I had never learned to quilt. I'd never grown a tomato or bean in my life. I didn't know how to turn peppers into hot sauce, had never cooked grits, and I wouldn't have recognized sugar cane without a clearly-marked nursery tag hanging from it. I hadn't shot a rattlesnake with a .22 either as both of those women had. It was obvious I'd come into this Southern family with serious deficiencies.

I guess I wouldn't have felt so bad if I'd had *some* homemaking skills. But I cremated my first roast because my mother-in-law assumed I knew to put water in a pressure cooker when she gave me the recipe. And baby skills? I had to call a friend for help changing my first cloth diaper.

In light of those domestic shortcomings, it must have seemed rather bold for me to have made such a strong statement to my in-laws on that fateful day back in 1982. Speeches like that set us up for future humility. Six years and two children later, I'd learned to cook, sew and even quilt, and had changed plenty of diapers. I'd even learned to shoot Bill's .22 and .38 (though I've still never shot a rattlesnake). But, my parenting skills were looking pretty shabby. My hoped-for "great kids" weren't even acting like "good kids" on some days!

> It was the beginning of being changed rather than requiring change, of winning our children's hearts rather than trying to shape them to a standard.

That year marked the beginning of a journey of the heart for me, where I began to submit to being changed rather than requiring change, and to winning our children's hearts rather than trying to shape them to a mold. As a result, I saw our "bad kids" make gradual shifts toward actually looking like "good kids." That was heartening!

But, only a few years later, I noticed that they were shifting again – this time from being "good kids" to actually looking like "great kids." The only major difference was that we'd replaced most of our extra-curricular activities with ministry. Our family began regularly 1) giving secretly to the poor, and 2) doing good works for the Lord where others could see (letting our lights shine).

I didn't know at the time we added those activities that we'd be changed by them. I was just looking for a worthy others-centered activity to plug in where our old me-centered extra-curricular activities had been.

Giving Alms

Sell what you have, and give alms; provide yourselves bags which do not grow old, a treasure in the heavens that does not fail, where no thief steals, nor do moths destroy. For where your treasure is, there will your heart be also. Luke 12:33

Giving alms is giving to the poor. In Luke 11 Jesus told the hypocritical Pharisees that all things would become clean to them if they would "*give alms of such things as you have....*" And in Acts 10 God chose Cornelius to be the first Gentile to be filled with the Holy Spirit because his "*prayers and alms are come up for a memorial before God.*"

When we tried to teach our children about becoming great by studying greatness, the result was head knowledge with little change of heart. When I took them to the food bank with me to buy groceries for low-income seniors, and then took them to knock on doors of the elderly with bags of food in their arms, and when we did that week after week – their hearts began to change. They began to experience greatness by becoming servants.

At the age of seventeen Mother Teresa gave herself to a life of poverty and service to the poor based on just one verse: "*Whatever you did to the least of these, you did to Me.*"[47] Amy Carmichael also exchanged comfort for poverty to serve the poor. Both these women and hundreds of missionaries like them loved to say that their sufferings didn't compare to the personal satisfaction and joy they experienced in serving the poor.

Our little family didn't give up everything to go to the mission field, but we have experienced a taste of that same joy by serving the poor in our own community. It was definitely scary to push myself out of my comfort zone, but it eventually got easier. And it became rewarding. Not only did I see we were making a difference in other people's lives, but I began to see a change in our family. At first we chatted about the people we served that day at the dinner table, rather than just talking about our own day. Later we started thinking about ways to add people to our list whenever we heard of a need. Pretty soon helping others became a way of life.

Something begins to happen inside us when we give to the poor in Jesus' name. I didn't even realize that my heart had been conditioned to insensitivity until it began to melt.

And when he had gone out into the street, a man came running, and kneeled before him, and asked him, "Good Master, what should I do to inherit eternal life?" And Jesus said to him, "Why do you call Me good? There is none good but one, that is, God. You know the commandments: Do not commit adultery. Do not kill. Do not steal. Do not bear false witness. Do not lie. Honor your father and mother." And he answered him, "Master, all these I have observed from my youth." Mark 10:17-20

I think any parent would be happy for their child to grow up like this young man. I know I would. He had observed God's commandments in his youth (sparing them difficult teen years). Luke 18 says he was a ruler, so he was enjoying a successful career. On top of having financial security, power and fame, he hadn't lost a zeal for spiritual things or his humility (he came running to Jesus, kneeling before Him).

Wow. What an influence for good this man probably was in his extended family, his business dealings, and his community. How blessed any nation would be to have all their leaders in such a spiritual condition. I could just imagine Jesus responding to him by saying, "Behold! A humble ruler who honors the commandments of My Father." After all, this man had just sincerely told Jesus Christ that he had observed God's commandments from his youth! And Jesus didn't contradict or rebuke him.

> Once we started experiencing the benefits of serving the poor, I saw it was about obeying God, about becoming more than just a follower, but a disciple.

And what a proud mother I would have been had that been my son. I could imagine Jesus turning to us and saying, "Well done," and perhaps I would blush and humbly say that we couldn't have done it without God's help. Then, I could see Jesus say to the young man, "Go and continue in your faithful service." And he would return home and perhaps start a personal ministry or a worthy organization, or a form a PAC[48] with other like-minded, devout civil leaders where he could make an ever bigger difference in the community.

Why didn't Jesus praise this productive, God-honoring, commandment-keeping, influential member of society? What more is there than obeying God's commandments? I'm *still* working on the first one!

Then Jesus beholding him loved him, and said to him, "One thing you lack. Go your way. Sell whatever you have, and give to the poor, and you shall have treasure in heaven. And come, take up the cross, and follow

Me." And he was sad at that saying, and went away grieved, for he had great possessions. Mark 10:21-22

Mark writes that Jesus, looking at this man, loved him. What a great picture, Jesus just looking at him, and Mark watching from the sidelines, recognizing a look we can only imagine, and then writing down later that He saw in that look – in just the look – that He loved him. Jesus then offered him the same deal, the same invitation He'd given the disciples: *Give up everything and follow Me.*

I used to think this passage was about not letting material comforts keep us from serving God. But once our family started experiencing the personal benefits of serving the poor, I saw it was also about a man who was sincerely obeying God's commands, but recognized something was lacking. Otherwise, he would never have come running to Jesus. This passage is also about becoming more than just a believer. It's about becoming a disciple.

I think that young man was sincere, but he'd gotten too comfortable with his gifts. And Jesus may have been quietly, kindly, lovingly communicating to this savvy businessman, "Look, I can see right into you. I know you are comfortable with your life and all its perks. But, you know it's not enough. Would you like to find the fulfillment your riches aren't giving you? Then give them all away. But, not forever. You'll just be rolling them over from this temporary market into an eternal investment. And the returns will be higher than you can imagine. If you can do that, if you can part with your prosperity here in order to receive something more there, then I'm inviting you to come with Me, and I'll show you more truth and love than you can possibly imagine."

One problem was that this man had much more to give up than the disciples. Selling all his possessions wouldn't just cost him great wealth and personal comfort; it would also cost him position and influence. He wasn't just being asked to walk away from a family business, but a career in public office, along with the prestige and power that went with it. When the "sticker shock" of what discipleship would cost hit him, he got scared and turned away. He probably could have bought anything his heart desired, but here was something he felt he couldn't afford. Oh, what he missed that day. It's for our own good that God asks us to give!

There are two things to remember when we give alms. First, we're supposed to do it *in* <u>secret</u>.

> *Take heed that you do not do your alms before men, to be seen by them, otherwise you have no reward from your Father who is in heaven. Therefore when you do your alms, do not sound a trumpet before you, as the hypocrites do in the synagogues and in the streets, that they may have glory from men. Truly I say unto you, they have their reward. But when you do alms, do not let your left hand know what your right hand is doing, so that your alms may be in secret. And your Father who sees in secret shall reward you openly Himself. Matthew 6:1-4*

Secondly, we're supposed to give with the right motivation of <u>love</u>.

And though I give all my goods to feed the poor...but do not have love, it profits me nothing. 1 Corinthians 13:3

If we give with selfish motivation, the poor still benefit – they still receive our goods! However, *we* won't profit. Our giving becomes little more than a social service. It really is for our own good that God asks us to give!

Good Works

Good works, on the other hand, can be done openly where they can be seen in order to bring glory to God. We can do good works for <u>people in the world</u>...

Let your light shine before men in such a way that they may see your good works and glorify your Father who is in heaven. Matthew 5:16

And we can do good works for <u>one another</u>...

Therefore, as we have opportunity, let us do good to all, especially to those who are of the household of faith." Galatians 6:10

If a brother or sister is naked and destitute of daily food, and one of you says to them, "Depart in peace, be warmed and filled," but you do not give them the things which are needed for the body, what does it profit? James 2:15-16

They only asked us to remember the poor – the very thing I was eager to do. Galatians 2:10

We can also do good works for our <u>neighbors</u>.

Which now of these three do your think was a neighbor to him that fell among the thieves? And he said, "He that showed mercy to him." Then Jesus said to him, "Go, and do likewise." Luke 10:36-3

Neighbors, it seems, would include people that God allows to cross our paths. They don't have to share our faith, just be in need of our assistance and compassion. We find them as we go along our way.

We're also to take care of <u>widows</u> and the <u>orphans</u>.

Pure religion and undefiled before God and the Father is this, to visit the fatherless and widows in their affliction. James 1:27

I'll never forget how uncomfortable I felt the first time I visited a nursing home with our adult Sunday School class years ago. Though I didn't realize it then, my fear was actually of what I would find in my own heart when facing the new and unknown world of the needy. I realized later that it was myself I was really afraid of. I didn't know how I would respond to the elderly and needy.

If the idea of helping people who are poor, hungry, lonely, handicapped or mentally-ill seems intimidating, or even frightening, then it's in allowing the Lord to reveal the reasons for those fears, one at a time and fear by fear, that He is able to deliver. This is another amazing way we are changed as we give of ourselves.

Nursing homes are filled with seniors who need and appreciate the warmth of a genuine smile and the touch of a child's hand.[49] Downtown apartment buildings are usually filled with seniors who appreciate food at the end of the month when their Social Security checks run out.

We're supposed to take care of our own families first,[50] though. Children can do good deeds for grandparents, even if it's just sending notes or pictures, hand-made cards, or calling and visiting. It may seem like it's one more thing to do in addition to all their schoolwork and our duties, but it brings a renewal which none of us can afford to live without.

> It's in allowing the Lord to reveal the causes for our fears that He is able to deliver us from them.

Our family didn't know anyone who was truly poor or needy until a friend at church introduced us to his food ministry.[51] Later we asked a city manager and a police officer who introduced us to several widows who lived nearby. Other families have asked for referrals from food banks, social services, churches, friends, family and neighbors.

The Physically Handicapped

> *But when you make a feast, call the poor, the maimed, the lame, the blind, and you shall be blessed; for they cannot repay you. For you shall be repaid at the resurrection of the just. Luke 14:13, 14*

When we first began serving the needy, we met a woman who was both very deformed and mentally handicapped. Because her face was so disfigured, it was hard for me to look at her, much less accept her into our lives. Even her child-like hugs of appreciation made me to stiffen.

One day when I was feeling particularly harsh and knew that if I could just have the heads of anyone within swinging range that I would feel better, a verse came to mind.

"...for the Lord sees not as man sees. For man looks on the outward appearance, but the Lord looks on the heart." 1 Samuel 16:7

I immediately felt like my inside was more hideous-looking than this deformed woman's outside, and that her inside was glorious and beautiful. I had been too blind to see. It was a life-changing revelation that I know I would never have experienced had I not allowed, even against my comfort-level, this poor, maimed individual into my life, and thereby into our children's lives. Since then, it's been easier to recognize that the ugliness from which I'm supposed to recoil, and from which I must teach my children to recoil, is self-centeredness and pride.

Give and it shall be given to you.[52]

While caroling at a nursing home with other families a nurse called over her shoulder, "You can't leave without singing to Queen. It will be such a blessing!" As we walked into Queen's room, I realized that she was completely paralyzed. I was so glad we had come. Queen joined us in singing, and then told us her story.

A drunk driver hit her car twenty-five years before, paralyzing her from the neck down. She had been in her early forties, still raising five children. As I listened to her story, I tried to imagine what it would be like for me, now in *my* early forties and still raising *my* children, to be suddenly disabled, unable to take care of anyone in my family. But, for the will of God, we could have traded places. The man who hit her walked away unharmed, but he had never called to ask about her or apologize. Yet, she told us that because of Jesus, she carried no unforgiveness or bitterness toward him. She then spoke these words to our children:

"Children, I'm just like you. I want to run and play and do all the things you do. I want to use my arms to pick up my grandchildren, to dial the phone, to call my daughter, to hug the neck of a friend. But I can't. And even though that's hard, I never feel sorry for myself. God has filled my heart with thankfulness to be alive. I thank each nurse who feeds me each day, each one who turns me, each one who helps me with every little thing because I am grateful to be alive.

"Don't you ever feel sorry for yourselves, no matter what may happen to you. There will always be those who have more trials, or have fewer things in this world than you do. But, we have the Lord, and we have life. And we have people who love us. You have your parents, and I have family that loves me, and there are some people that don't have that. None of us are allowed more trials than we can bear.

"My, how you children have blessed me today! You've shown me that you cared enough about me to come and sing to me today. You have made my day so special by your coming! I am so thankful that you did!"

That nurse had been right. It had been "such a blessing." But, *we* were the ones who had been blessed. My posture as I walked into Queen's room that day had been that of the giver. Twenty minutes later, I walked out the receiver. This beautiful woman had given the greater blessing, and she passed it to us, word-by-word, heart-to-heart and life-to-life.

I took with me that day the most beautiful gift anyone gave to me that Christmas, and I'm still opening it, day by day. It was the gift of a grateful heart. I unwrapped it again later that day when our large van (with broken power steering) got stuck between two parking places in the nursing home parking lot *(Thank you, Lord, that we even have a van to drive. I know there are those who don't!),* and later when our preschooler had to make yet another bathroom stop *(Thank you, Lord, that he's healthy. I know there are mothers who would give much to trade places with me today!),* and later when standing in a slow line at the grocery store *(Thank you, Lord, that I can even stand in a line, and have money for food, and am healthy, and can know You and love You),* and right now, when it's late at night, and I'm tired of doing edits on this manuscript, and I would much rather crawl into my soft bed *(Thank you, Lord, that I even have lessons about You to share!).*

Besides that beautiful gift, I learned a powerful lesson about showing great respect to those we go to serve and being teachable. I had assumed we knew the Lord more closely than most of those we went to visit. After all, we were there by choice, not need. I was surprised to see how much I could learn – *if I were humble enough to listen.*

Compassion is stepping out of my own thoughts about my own schedule and commitments and needs, and stepping into someone else's world, imagining what it would be like to live in their world with their sorrows and pain, and hurting with them. The more we work with seniors, the more I realize that in just a few years I will be old, too. There we all will be, aged and weak and more vulnerable than we've ever been in our lives, and in more need of compassionate and respectful care than ever before. Humility is a low door that allows in many gifts. One of those gifts is great compassion.

> Compassion is stepping out of my own world and stepping into someone else's, imagining what it would be like to live in their world with their sorrows and pain.

Did I say I was doing this for our *children's* sake? The most effective way to change our children is by being changed ourselves! I had new curriculum to teach and shared my lessons with them. We all took this new understanding with us to the rest of our nursing home visits. It's a more humble perspective which turns what could quickly become a duty or a burden, or even a pride-filled work of vanity, into a looked-forward-to joy whenever we go.

Serving Leaders

Put them in mind to be subject to principalities and powers, to obey magistrates, <u>to be ready to every good work.</u> Titus 3:1

Serving others with right motives is an overriding quality in a truly great leader. And being "ready to every good work" can be as simple as helping civil leaders to do their jobs better.

Serving leaders can also be the most tempting of all good works, since the people our children serve may end up in positions to repay them. Invitations to special or private events, a recommendation for a job, or a future beneficial contact can be very appealing. But self-serving motivations will cloud our children's service, and rob them of the greater reward. Most leaders, and especially politicians, are savvy enough to sense when self-ambition is dressing itself up as good works. Works with personal motivations are just works. *Good* works are humbly doing whatever is needed, with the motivation of pleasing the Lord. It's expecting nothing in return.

Something also began to happen to our family when we felt like we were becoming a "part of the answer," even as small as our part was: the temptation to complain or joke about the failures of civil leaders was lessened. Again, our experience was that first we gave of ourselves and then our hearts began to change.

If I were to write a book on good works (which I'm not – I'm only testifying to what happened to us when we began to practice good works), I think I'd place limits on those to whom our works could be given. Those limitations would ensure that those people were in some qualifying way, deserving of my time and efforts. I would want to guarantee that my investment in them was worthwhile. Jesus, knowing that we'd be tempted to turn away from people we felt were undeserving, gave us such a guarantee when He promised, "Truly I say to you, 'In as much as you have done it to one of the least of these my brethren, you have done it to Me.'"[53]

We wouldn't put our children at physical or moral risk to help others, though. As a mom, I don't pick up hitchhikers, expose our children to the homeless or strangers on the street, or jeopardize their safety or health by subjecting them to communicable or questionable diseases. Other safeguards we practice include:

- Pray first for direction for the ministry the Lord would have for your family.
- Also pray for deliverance from evil, as Jesus taught us in the Lord's Prayer.
- Wash hands before and after visiting a nursing home. Seniors and children are more susceptible to germs.
- Deliver food to higher-risk areas such as downtown buildings where seniors live, during the day, when dads can join in, with other moms and children two-families-by-two, or three families-by-three - but not alone.
- Remind children that they shouldn't slip into strangers' homes or apartments without a parent even if they're invited, and that even we parents don't enter strangers' homes simply because we're invited.
- Carry a cell phone at all times and keep it turned on.

If our good works cause others to depend on us when they are able to fulfill their own God-given responsibilities, then our service could be more hindrance than help. However, when there are those whose lives are filled with the consequences of their own past sins and they are unable physically, emotionally or mentally to fulfill their responsibilities, then we must see these needs as opportunities to not only glorify God, but also be changed by God through them. God would have us all learn mercy.

> *And it came to pass, as Jesus sat at to eat in the house, behold, many publicans and sinners came and sat down with him and his disciples. And when the Pharisees saw it, they said to his disciples, "Why does your Master eat with publicans and sinners?" But when Jesus heard that, he said to them, "They that are healthy do not need a physician, but they that are sick. But you go and learn what this means, "<u>I will have mercy</u>, and not sacrifice." For I have not come to call the righteous, but sinners to repentance. Matthew 9:10-13*

Raising *great* kids takes a lot of physical, emotional, mental and spiritual energy. If we use our energy pouring out too many good works *on* our children, it can be to their detriment. The result will be a child-centered home that produces self-centered children who experience conflicts outside the home when life no longer revolves around them. The energy that it takes for parents to dig their children out from under the weight of self-indulgence can be daunting.

Doing what is best is not doing *for* them things they can do on their own, but instead teaching them how to first take care of themselves, and then let them join us in taking care of others. This type of parenting gives our children a healthy dose of reality that can make them better functioning family members and more responsible future citizens.

Our home should be a place that provides training in how to succeed in a world that doesn't revolve around any one person. By teaching younger ones to unload a dishwasher, set a table, put away their own clothes, we make the home the rightful center of all good works and charitable service. True, their motivations start out as only to obey us, but as they come to know the Lord, we encourage them to shift their motivations to pleasing the Lord.

> Our home should be a place that provides training in how to succeed in a world that doesn't revolve around any one person.

When our children were all little, it was difficult to do much of anything outside the home. For everything there is a season, but if we seek the Lord's direction, He can show us if there is somewhere that our families can serve. On rare occasions I've arranged playtime for a preschooler with another family while the older children and I served in a way that required more attention from me than I could give to both serving and toddler. Of course, if my preschooler can't yet behave well enough to be under a friend or relative's direction for a short while, then my first priority is to remain at home and continue to train him (that is one of my primary good works) and try to send the older children out to serve with another family.

We battle the philosophy of this world which says, "Nice guys finish last!" with truths such as, "The first shall be last, and the last shall be first,"[54] and, "If you want to be great in the Kingdom of God, you must be the servant of all."[55] The truth is, though, that "nice guys" often do finish last – here. That was the truth that the young man in Luke 18 missed. His wealth (and the perks it provided) blinded him to anything beyond the here and now.

The true purpose of doing good works is not to wipe out poverty or hunger[56] or to win that campaign (we should pray for and respect whichever leader is in office),[57] but to let our good works (for Jesus) so shine before men that we glorify our Father who is in Heaven. Our true purpose is to serve Him in all we do.

There is a higher purpose for our children than just blossoming in their accomplishments. We need to give them a higher vision, but we have to show them how to go lower to find the higher.

We begin by asking the Lord for His leading. And service projects such as charitable deeds and Scriptural good works are the very best ways to develop and nurture wise friendships for our children – which happens to be in the very next chapter!

Mother Teresa on Good Works

At the end of our lives, we will not be judged by how many diplomas we have received, how much money we have made or how many great things we have done. We will be judged by, "I was hungry and you gave me to eat. I was naked and you clothed me. I was homeless and you took me in." Hungry not only for bread, but hungry for love. Naked not only for clothing, but naked of human dignity and respect...this is Christ in distressing disguise.

Many people are talking about the poor, but very few people talk to the poor.

All we do - our prayer, our work, our suffering - is for Jesus. Our life has no other reason or motivation. This is a point many people do not understand. I serve Jesus twenty-four hours a day. Whatever I do is for Him. And He gives me the strength. I love Him in the poor and the poor in Him, but always the Lord comes first.

We must not drift away from the humble works, because these are the works nobody will do. It's never too small. We are so small and we look at things in a small way. But God, being Almighty, sees everything great. Therefore, even if you write a letter for a blind man or you just go and listen, or you take the mail for him, or you visit somebody or bring a flower to somebody - small things - or wash clothes for somebody, or clean the house - very humble work - that is where you and I must be. For there are many people who can do big things. But there are very few people who will do the small things.[58]

Do It Anyway by Mother Teresa

People are often unreasonable, illogical, and self-centered;
Forgive them anyway.

If you are kind,
People may accuse you of selfish, ulterior motives;
Be kind anyway.

If you are successful,
You will win some false friends and some true enemies;
Succeed anyway.

If you are honest and frank, people may cheat you;
Be honest and frank anyway.

What you spend years building,
Someone could destroy overnight; Build anyway.

If you find serenity and happiness,
They may be jealous;
Be happy anyway.

The good you do today,
People will often forget tomorrow;
Do good anyway.

Give the world the best you have, and it may never be enough;
Give the world the best you've got anyway.

You see, in the final analysis, it's between you and God;
It was never between you and them anyway.

Preface to Chapter Nine: A Letter to Wives

*A*ll of the things I share in the previous chapters of this book can be applied in a wife's life without a husband's cooperation – except the next chapter, *Under the Influence.* Chapter Nine is written by both Bill and me, and describes major decisions in the family that consequently require a husband to enforce if there is to be much hope of long-term success in those areas.

I encourage you to bypass the next chapter, especially if, like me, you have a tendency to compare, or if your relationship with your husband, or the Lord, is not where you want it to be. My experience has been that if I focus on standards in the home I think have to change (rather than my own heart) that I'm tempted to push him to take action or I take the lead myself. Or I allow the issues to become more important than my relationship with the Lord or with him. I then find that I lose more ground with our children, and do more damage to my marriage, than would have ever occurred had I simply yielded to his decision (or indecision), informed or not, on whatever issue was on the table. There is also the other rigid extreme of legalistically burdening a man with numerous, small decisions, many of which he may prefer to delegate, and later blaming him for "his decisions" when problems arise.

Children will naturally test the parental unity of new decisions (especially if those decisions remove a freedom they once had). Without the conviction and long-range stand of the father, it won't be long before a wife will react or buckle under the additional pressure of enforcing a new rule or standard by herself.

Since I'm of Choleric temperament (able to lead), with the Spiritual gift of prophecy (seeing issues as black and white/right or wrong), and function as a high-achieving firstborn, I've spent many years wanting to "help" my Phlegmatic (laid-back, slow to change) husband, whose Spiritual gift is serving (joyfully behind-the-scenes making others successful), and whose first-born tendency is his dependability.

Since it's expensive to learn from our mistakes, but cheap to learn from others' mistakes, I share the most important lesson that I have learned about raising children of character with you wonderful, precious moms who only want what is best for your children and families: It's this: If we want to teach our children how to trust God and how to love us, even when they don't think that we, as their God-given authorities, are making the best decisions for their lives – then we must learn how to trust God and to love our husband, as our God-given authority, even when we don't believe that he is making the best decisions for our lives. We can tell our children to trust God when they disagree with us over a decision, but they will learn by what they see us do. Children learn by example.

> If I focus on standards I think have to change, rather than on my own heart, issues become more important than my relationship with the Lord, or with my husband.

That may sound discouraging. To me it meant death. Death to many hopes and dreams that I had for my children, for me, for my husband, and for our family. It didn't seem fair. After I no longer pined for the nicer house, the easier life, or the more spiritual self, what could be wrong with wanting only God's best in our lives? *Why*, I thought, *would God withhold such a good request? And how could He be more interested in my response to my husband, than in the issues that were affecting us?* But, it is in those responses, the reflection of our inner motivations, that He does His greatest work.

Dying to self is not the same as resignation or manipulation or indifference or rigid compliance. It's not just dying to the pleasures of life; it's dying to *everything*, good or bad, that we want more than knowing Christ. The apple that Eve desired was *good*. What is wrong with wanting something beautiful that would also make her wise? But to gain wisdom we don't step out from under authority as Eve regrettably discovered. If we have to step out from under authority to get something good, it becomes bad once we get it. Eve needed to trust her God.

Dying to self is not even possible in our own strength. So, if we find that we are not willing to die, we can cry out to God to help us to become willing. We have to invite Him to thrust the knife into our dreams; He will not do so unless we ask. That is a wonderful, yet terrifying place to be. It's a place of rest and trust, where it becomes blatantly obvious that spirituality begins with obedience to God no matter what, that marriage is the primary relationship in the family, that God loves our children more than we do, and that He truly sees our struggles and is working all things together for good. No one can teach us about that place; we have to go there on our own. We have to die to everything except Christ.[59]

I could write about the sweet things that can take place after that death, but they are best discovered personally. To die, giving God permission to give nothing in return for our hearts and our wills is a most costly sacrifice, but it brings many different rewards.

Chapter Nine: Under the Influence
of Friends, Peers, Television, Music, Media and More...

Every man whose tastes have been allowed to develop in wrong directions, or in whom the best tastes have failed of higher perfection, loses thereby from the inner joy and outer value of his whole life. Every good taste is a source and guarantee of happy healthy hours and days, and thus of the enrichment and elevation of life. A reasonable capacity to appreciate music and art quite suffices to enrich life and exercise a wholesome influence upon character. The taste for good reading is inseparable from a taste for good thinking.
Edward O. Sisson[60]

Friends

Iron sharpens iron; so a man sharpens the countenance of his friend. Proverbs 27:17

Friends can have such a strong influence in our lives, either for good or for bad. How many times in our own past have we been encouraged or discouraged, grown wiser or been hindered, made right choices or wrong choices – while "driving under the influence" of friends.

We are all influenced by the company we keep. It's hard for all of us to pull away from those whom we love or admire, to follow a different path – especially if that path looks strange to our friends! Decisions as a young person, even decisions as an adult about our families, our children, or educational choices we make for our children can cause us all to feel the pull, even if only in our own minds, from those whose friendships we cherish. The "Baaah" factor (that pull to do what the rest of the flock is doing, and the good feelings and security we get from being the same as other sheep) is felt by even those most dedicated to following purely the Shepherd's call. The closer the friend (or the closer we want someone to become), the more influence he can have on our desires and our decisions. Being able to sense and identify that pull can help us to discern whether the pressure that we feel about a particular decision is coming from our beliefs, or from our need to bond with, or to maintain the approval of friends.

Being able to identify the influence our own friends have had on us helps us to understand the power of influence of our children's friends. How important it is that we win and keep our children's hearts, so that their desire to please us, and the Lord, remains stronger than the pull to fit in with (and please) their friends. We are supposed to mature; they (and their friends) are supposedly less mature. We are supposed to have our children's best in mind at the cost of personal sacrifice; their friends normally wouldn't have our child's best in mind, at the cost of personal sacrifice.

It's obvious that young children need our protection and guidance in many areas until they are mature enough to choose what is right on their own. If it has ever been difficult for us to stand by our own convictions when surrounded by those we care about who didn't understand or agree with us, we should be able to understand how difficult it can be for our children. In addition, our children have not yet established their place in society, and are more susceptible to the lure of social acceptance and approval – especially when placed in a group setting.

Good friendships are developed one by one, not in groups. Children may have a large circle of acquaintances, but they don't need a large circle of friends. Even as adults, with all of our varied temperaments, if we find a few close friends we count ourselves blessed. One good friend, whose heart is also turned toward his parents and the Lord, is more beneficial to our child than many acquaintances. This is true especially for the Sanguine temperament child, who thinks he must have many friends to survive. Because of his strong tendency to please people, though, it's better for him to have many acquaintances, but only a few good friends.

Children need positive influences and safe boundaries until they are mature enough to govern themselves in the middle of negative influences with no boundaries. That kind of maturity doesn't come with age so much as with training. Training happens as we let our children know what right behavior is and how pleased we are for them when they make right choices, and then provide small settings for them to put into practice what they have learned. If they govern themselves rightly in the small settings for a while, then we can slowly widen their social circle, always encouraging them and praising them for character growth. However, we wouldn't put children into social settings for the sake of socialization, or into any situation where they might find themselves "over their head" in temptation – especially if their failure could mean devastating or long-term results.

If they have trouble standing for what's right in the smaller settings, then we lovingly draw them back in "under our wing" for more training, or just to wait until they become more emotionally mature. Character is being able to be true to one's conscience – whether all alone, in the family, in the church, or in the world.

There are three types of friendships we can help our children to develop: discipleship, iron-sharpening-iron, and ministry.

> Character is being true to one's conscience whether all alone, in the family, in the church, or in the world.

Discipleship Friendships: Being Influenced by Others for Good

I am a companion of all that fear You, and of those that keep Your precepts. Psalms 119:63

When our children were young, we met a family with three biological children and eight adopted children. What struck me immediately was not their family size, but their love for one another. The teens showed tender care for their younger siblings and such love for the Lord and their parents. Their interaction with each other gave me hope for our children. Over the following weeks, and then years, I pursued that family. We asked if they could drive up for dinner (we'd provide the food), if we could drive down for dinner (we'd provide the food), if we could help them work on their house (we'd provide the labor), if our children could spend time with their children (we'd provide the transportation). Why did I pursue them so? The mom demonstrated the character that I had been struggling to develop, and her children's character was where we wanted our children's character to one day be. We began a being-discipled friendship with them and their children began an "influencing for good" friendship with our children. The mom never sat down and taught me, but she discipled me by letting me spend time with her. I learned by watching her example. And our children were positively influenced by her children as they worked and played together.

Be followers of me, even as I also am of Christ.
I Corinthians 11:1

How beneficial it was for our family to develop a friendship with a family that had the type of character strengths we wanted to see in our own. If children's gender or ages don't match, or if personalities don't quite mesh, just keep praying and keep looking. We sometimes offer to have someone else's child accompany us, or we send a self-governing child along with another family, when whole families are unable to get together. And when we do pursue a friendship where we know we will be on the receiving end, we try to offer the practical things that will make it work, like food and transportation, along with intangibles like flexibility and appreciation.

Iron-Sharpening-Iron Friendships: Encouraging One Another to Do Good

Iron sharpens iron, so a man sharpens the countenance of his friend. Proverbs 27:17

Finding other children (usually one at a time) who are our child's age and gender, whose character and maturity are similar, and who live within a reasonable distance can take a few tries. Asking the Lord for wisdom and help is the first step. Inviting another child or his family on a ministry opportunity or on a service project is a good way to start. There is a lot to be said for building friendships around ministry. Taking food to needy families, visiting the elderly in nursing homes, helping with someone's house repair or building project, or team-teaching younger children are all activities that children can do with friends.

The possibilities for mixing ministry and friendships are endless. During an election year our children are quite busy meeting friends – at a campaign office making signs together, at friends' houses stuffing mailers, on the campaign trail roller-blading through subdivisions and pounding in yard signs.

It's a good idea to observe the character and maturity of the children rather than the parents when we're trying to find friends for our children. Most parents have worthy goals, but sometimes can't see their children's problems. It's the *children's* maturity that we consider, not their parents'. If we find that our child's friend is not as mature as we thought, then maybe our child can develop a ministry friendship with him.

Ministry Friendships: Influencing Others for Good

But exhort one another daily, while it's called today, lest any of you be hardened through the deceitfulness of sin. Heb 3:13

When a child has learned to govern himself in the home, and then outside the home with like-minded friends, he might be ready to have a ministry friendship with those whose character and standards are not the same as his. The caution on this, obviously, is that if the swing in values is too great, if we invite more than one friend at a time, if we leave them alone for too long, or if our child is not as mature as we expected, then weaker friends could do more harm than good. Carefully explaining and encouraging our child in the types of attitudes and behaviors we expect, and praising him for small successes goes a long way toward curbing urges to impress a friend. If our child can bring violations of house rules or other cautions to our attention when it's appropriate, without an attitude of judgment toward his friend, we know that his heart is still turned toward pleasing us. If he covers his friend's misdeeds, his heart may be turning toward pleasing him, or he might be giving in to fear of judgment by his friend. If he tattles for the pleasure of getting his friend in trouble, he has an underdeveloped sense of security, and we can encourage and help him in that area. But, if he's learning to stand firm in his own choices, and let us know if friends are secretly disobeying house rules without judging his friends, he is on his way to Christian maturity. Our child's behavior, overseen and praised by us, can have an influencing-for-good effect on his friends.

Socialization

He that walks with wise men shall be wise, but a companion of fools shall be destroyed. Proverbs 13:20

Socialization (that dreaded "S" word) was the buzzword in the early years of homeschooling, when it was unknown whether our children would be able to function in the "real world" if they were not saturated in peer interaction. But, the controlled environment of the age-segregated classroom and campus is not at all like the real world. And socialization only *measures* maturity; it doesn't teach it. The overwhelming evidence shows that home educated children are more socially adjusted than their public schooled counterparts.[61]

Interpersonal skills, such as how to choose and keep good friends, are best learned and practiced in the home, and then widened to include others. To expect healthy interaction to develop through socialization is like expecting children to learn to swim by throwing them into the deep end of a pool en masse. Some will get it; some will drown. Some will learn to stay afloat by pushing others down. They can then convince others that they are really "swimming," thereby influencing those who are struggling to stay afloat to imitate their behavior, no matter what a coach may be shouting from the pool's edge.

Socialization first/maturity later approaches life backward. We would no sooner throw our children into the deep end of the pool to teach them to swim than give them the car keys and tell them to just start driving – when they hit a few cars, or people, they will learn from their experiences. Socialization-first is even more dangerous because the dangers are greater, but can't be recognized by the eye – children may be wounded and bleeding and dying inside but a parent can totally miss it or misjudge it. And socialization, especially before a child can choose conscience over peer pressure, almost always has negative consequences. Exposure doesn't produce skills; it just gives a place to practice them. Socialization, then, is not a need or a right; it's a litmus test of maturity.

The sliding state of public-schooled youth testifies to the harm in grouping children, who by nature are immature, together with their peers day after day, year after year, where success is often defined as social acceptance and performance. That strong social influence, intensified in the bonds of friendship, can do more to change the course of a child's life than all of the education, insight and warning in the world.

> Strong social influence, intensified in the bonds of friendship, can do more to change the course of a child's life than all of the education, insight and warning in the world.

Group Activities

Group socialization in the Christian or homeschool community presents the same socialization pitfalls as the public schools, but on a smaller scale. Unless the directors or teachers are committed to keeping the hearts of the children turned to their parents and to the Lord, and to returning those children who can't govern themselves (or their attitudes) to their parents, the overall character of the group will usually slide. It may slide little or it may slide much. Sliding little is actually more dangerous; it's akin to slowly bringing a lobster to boil – the change is so gradual that by the time it realizes it's in hot water, it's cooked.

A youth group or co-op environment in which the overall character of the group is not as high as a family's, tempts children to acclimate to that slightly lower standard rather than face opposition for "minor issues." Children are not mature enough to differentiate between shades of gray when they are still learning the foundations of what is black and white. Pressure to conform within the friendlier environment of the youth group, support group or co-op is greater than the pressure to conform to the world, because it's with those groups that our children most identify and feel the strongest need to stay secure.

That doesn't mean that our children never participate in group activities. However, before a child goes into any activity where children outnumber adults, we evaluate whether he's responsive to us, and to his own conscience at home. If he has character problems at home, he'll take them with him wherever he goes. If he *does* behave better for others than he does for us, that's not a sign of maturity. It just means he's placed more value on others' opinions of him than ours, or that he's learned that certain behavior has certain immediate rewards. To be a good participant (a good guest, a good friend, a good fellow student) he should be able to choose what's right over what he wants.

If he is responsive to us and to his conscience, we then evaluate the purpose of that activity. Opportunities for children today abound, so narrowing it down to the best can be a challenge. We ask the Lord for wisdom, and typically choose ministry opportunities over educational ones (though not always). It's also a good idea to check our own motives, and to be alert to our own temptations as well. It's natural for us to want our children to *do* their best in those activities, but it's far better to teach them to *be* their best while they are there.

We then evaluate the costs. Would the skill or benefit he would gain from the activity outweigh the costs to the rest of the family in lost family time or dinners or evenings together? How would it affect other family members with transportation or financial needs? How much parental support would be needed to help him with the activity or volunteer support with the group? Everything costs something, and when children participate in more than one outside the home activity, there can be major costs. The highest cost is usually for mom, who, in addition to everything else, now finds herself transporting children back and forth between various lessons, activities and events, and then volunteering to make some of those activities successful as well. In addition, when one child participates in an activity, it usually creates pressure for siblings to also choose an activity. Moms can face burnout before long, simply from chauffeuring, volunteering and preparation for outside the home activities! More subtle costs are in missed meals together, pressure-filled evenings working on project or assignment deadlines, and less time to work on issues of the heart with our children. In addition, children need free time to play and rest and just be children!

If the overall benefit looks like it will outweigh the costs, and we will be attending the activity with him, we give clear expectations of what good social behavior is, and of course, we expect him to make mistakes as he learns. It's his attitude that we watch. Is his attention drawn more toward pleasing his peers or following our direction? If we sense a wall going up between our child and us, if we see that he's not governing himself, if he begins to show signs of pride or rebellion or self-centeredness or ungratefulness, if he becomes aloof or contentious, if influence of friends begins to overshadow instruction of parents, or if we see the roots of other character flaws taking hold in his life, how unwise to encourage and facilitate his growth in the skill of that activity at a faster rate than his character is growing!

Keeping the hearts of our children turned toward us and toward the Lord, so they don't slip into needing peers' approval, can be challenging. It's important to remember that only God can truly change a heart; we are only His instruments. But as His instruments, we can speak truth in love, and do His works of love to protect, win and keep our children's hearts for Him. We want to train our child to govern himself within the home, before we expect him to govern himself in a social setting.

If we won't be attending the activity with him, and he's self-governing, then we try to evaluate the maturity and attitudes of the other children or youth in that activity. If others will be participating whom we know have the same root problems as our child, or with problems that we believe would cause him to stumble, we don't expect him to function at a level of maturity in which he isn't currently walking. Children, like adults, can only be salt when they keep their savor. They lose their savor when their conscience is "trampled under foot by peers." If heavy peer dependence exists within the group, and it's obvious that our child would be considered an outsider, he'd have to be very mature to derive the benefit of the activity knowing that he'd have to live without peer acceptance. And to do so without ill feelings toward those who exclude or judge him would be very mature, indeed. If it's more probable that he may be accepted by the group, but we know that he has difficulty choosing conscience over peers now, it would be unwise to put him into an environment of heavy peer influence. We don't want to put temptations in front of our child in the areas of his weakness. Compatibility with peers through conformity is weakness, but loving peers while choosing what is right is strength. This is where we want our children to be as soon as we can lovingly get them there. By the time children are walking in this level of character, their pull toward career and ministry-focused opportunities leads the way, and only the conflicts on the calendar (and keeping up with necessary studies) hold them back. Group socialization is not a right of childhood, but a good friend is a blessing.

Youth Groups

When Jon was about twelve, we kept him from entering the church youth group. While we were grateful to be making such good strides in regaining his heart, we could see that he was still not governing himself with enough maturity to warrant more independence. We had also been challenged to find a Scriptural mandate for a youth group or youth ministry, and had been impressed by our "discipleship" family's teens who had bypassed youth groups and were so close to their siblings and parents.

> Children lose their savor when their conscience is "trampled under foot by peers."

It was a difficult decision to make, and it was difficult for Jon to make the break from his friends, some of whom he had known since the age of four. He was being forced to "walk alone," away from the rest of his only set of friends, in which he had already built some security, for a conviction that his parents (with whom he was still occasionally conflicting) had newly embraced, while he was still struggling with his own conscience. It was hard for him, and for me. I had unknowingly been building security of my own on friendships and accepted traditions, and was beginning to feel the "Baaah" factor myself.

Recently some friends asked us about taking their thirteen year-old son out of the youth group. Jon's reply to those parents was written when he was nineteen, still young enough to remember the costs of walking alone, but old enough to have experienced some of the benefits. Here is a portion of his reply:

If you pull your son away from the normal youth group activities, he will suffer. But helping him to see a higher purpose for his trials will make all the difference. In order to do this, though, it helps a great deal if you first make sure that you understand your son's needs and wants. I'm not that far out of childhood, and I can tell you that it's quite true that people in general, and children especially, will not be interested in what you have to say until they are sure that you understand their position.

Your son is naturally going to want to be with his friends and to have some fellowship with people his own age. He might feel afraid of being different, or of leaving a position in which he feels secure. Whatever his feelings on the matter are, if you can listen without judging it will create a secure environment in which he will be able to give weight to your ideas. Give him the space to respectfully state his views and communicate his feelings to you.

Having done that…give him a vision of what God's best is. It's extremely important for him to understand why the majority of what he would be exposed to in a youth group is not God's best. It's important for you to understand, too, in case you aren't sure. You are going to receive opposition, possibly from good friends with whom you've always felt a oneness before, and it will be tempting to give in to that pressure and go with the flow if you aren't basing your decision on the solid conviction that what you are doing is best, no matter what anyone else says

To give purpose to the problems that your son is going to face, you need to instill in him the desire to have God's best for his life, rather than something that is merely good. The activities that you mentioned in your email are all either neutral or good…God's ideal within the church is that we serve one another in love (John 13:14). Jesus said that the servant of all would be the greatest. (Matt.20:26). So, whom are these activities really serving? After the day of service to the church, all that is left are some purely recreational activities and seven fundraisers for a youth trip to listen to music and speakers with 1000 other teens…It's my strong opinion that children, even teens, weren't meant to be put together in large, age-segregated groups for any significant amount of time. There is no Scriptural basis for it, and my personal experience leads me to the conclusion that it's not a profitable practice.

I enjoy getting together with friends for games…but the focus of a church-related activity should be to shine a light to the world (Matt.5:13-16), to serve one another (John 13:14), and to exhort one another (Heb. 3:13), not to play games. To anyone who would say that fun activities are a means of encouragement and exhortation, my response would be, "You've never been discouraged." When someone needs spiritual encouragement, paint ball and golf don't get it done. Encouragement involves serious listening, empathy, Scripture searching and prayer that lifts the spirits of all who hear. I know this because it's real; I've been there and done it. You can't do any real spiritual work while trading paintball shots. You can have fun, though. Just don't try to dress it up as a worthwhile spiritual activity.

What I'm trying to get at is that what normally goes on in youth groups…can be "good."…But frankly, not many people are impressed with Christians who are merely "good." They've got the main convictions that offend the world (abstinence until marriage, not getting drunk, no drugs, no profanity, no sensuality) but few of the convictions that come from a life lived with a willingness to suffer for what's best.

The Army and the Navy have recently struggled to meet their recruitment requirements, but the Marines have no trouble filling their ranks. A buzz cut and a scholarship is a buzz cut and a scholarship, you say. What's the difference? The Marines are the best, and they stand by their convictions. Standards aren't dropped to make people feel good. Their main selling point is the pursuit of pain and a willingness to suffer to be the best. "Pain is weakness leaving the body," say their recruitment posters, next to a picture of a soldier grimacing as he struggles to make the next ladder rung. Young people flock to the Marines. The majority of the world would flock to a church that had the courage to be the kind of believers God wants us to be: the best. The majority of the world also laughs at people who have nothing to offer except rules they don't like and trips to play golf. Can we blame them?

What should replace the youth group? A higher goal.

Jesus said to love one another and to serve; He humbled Himself and took on the form of a servant in order to show us the way. There are needy people all around us: the elderly, the widows, and the disabled to name a few. Even people we don't normally think of as "needy" have needs that aren't being met. Show your son that the loss of the entertaining activities of the youth group is nothing compared to the joy of helping someone who really needs it…Compare this to the feeling we would have from doing a fundraiser carwash so that we could have a fun trip with our friends. You can encourage your son to invite a couple of his youth group friends to join him in service projects. They can always have fun afterwards, of course. There's also nothing wrong with having friends over just to have fun, by the way. But seeing who will serve by his side without complaining can be an important way for your son to find out who his real friends should be. The ones who don't show and the ones who don't come back are the ones with whom it isn't worth developing the closest relationships. The ones who have a servant's heart are people he'll want to pursue.

Around the age of twelve, there was pressure on my parents to put me into the youth group. They found an area of the church where I could serve on Sunday mornings while my peers were in the youth group: serving the nursery and children's Sunday School workers. I would deliver the snacks and the record books, and then go back

> _____
> Show your son that the loss of the entertaining activities of the youth group is nothing compared to the joy of helping someone who really needs it.
> _____

and pick up the empty containers and the completed books. Pushing a loud, rattling snack cart down the halls of the church to the stares (and questions) of people my parents knew while everyone else I knew was playing games and having fun over in the youth hall wasn't cool. It was embarrassing, and at the time, it hurt…I was a little bit lonely.

In retrospect, however, I was gaining everything and losing nothing worth having in the first place. Here's why: one of my few consolations on the snack route was the engaging conversations I had with the husband of the woman who ran the nursery and Sunday School program. This was the very beginning of a value for adult input and perspectives that has never left me. Because of the decision by my parents to keep me out of the peer group, I was protected for a few years from the pressure cooker of peer pressure. Instead of caring what my peer group thought, my views were being formed by a wiser and more mature group: Christian adults. Later, as I served as a 4-H camp counselor, I had to learn to stand by my convictions (and my parent's convictions, where mine were lower) where my peers were concerned, even when it hurt. Principles carry over into the next stage of life, and the next, and the next, and the next. I recently had to turn down a job offer I wanted very badly because I would have had to work a few hours one Sunday a month.

The ability to set aside what you want for what's right isn't going to be learned in a youth group, where conformity to the group and comfort dictate standards. This was all in addition to the fact that I was learning to serve others rather than myself. The lesson carried over into all other aspects of my life. The first thing that comes to mind when presented with a new situation is, "How can

I serve these people?" All of this would have been lost if my parents had gone with the flow, or thrown in the towel when the youth pastor or others disagreed with them.

When you decided to home educate your children, you were probably viewed skeptically by some friends and family members, but you stayed the course. Your children are now academically and socially far more advanced. This will be a similar situation with similar difficulties. It might even be harder for you, since the criticism will be mostly coming from within the church, rather than from the world. But, as with your educational choices, you will be proven right in the end. You just need to know it and not forget it when the going gets tough.

Jon Freeman

Jon spent his free time during middle and high school accelerating his studies, devouring great books, volunteering for numerous service projects, and having lots of fun with his family and family friends. They were years were filled with SCUBA diving, hunting, mountain hiking, white-water rafting, camping, canoeing, sailing and just playing. He learned numerous practical skills fixing things around our house, passed college CLEP[62] exams at sixteen, and was accepted to a Christian distance-learning law school at eighteen.

His younger siblings have not experienced the same "pulling away" that he did, however, since we were in the process of "finding our way" and changing our direction with our "lab-rat" firstborn. In many ways, he paved the way for them.

Music

Brethren, be not children in understanding. However, in malice be children, but in understanding be men. 1 Corinthians 14:20

We were sitting under a big, beautiful oak tree, Bill and I, on a gorgeous fall afternoon. The air was balmy, the company perfect, and I should have been able to enjoy it. But I couldn't. I was agitated and upset. We had just listened to a Christian leader articulate on why he thought it was unwise to mix the message of the gospel with rock-and-roll music.

"Well, I don't agree with him!" I nearly shouted. I knew that Bill wouldn't agree either, because we both had been deeply influenced by Keith Green's music for years. To think that this leader was spreading that message as though it were the "gospel" really irritated me. Bill finished his drink and looked over at me in his typical "Clark Kent" non-reactionary style.

"Okay," he smiled. But he smiled in a way that made me think all might not be "Okay." I looked at him suspiciously.

Character is who we are when our opinions are challenged.

"Okay? Is that all you have to say?" I ventured. "You certainly don't agree with that, do you?"

He took another drink, and then paused again, obviously in deep thought.

"I think I do." He stated this evenly, without emotion. The company didn't look so perfect anymore.

"How can you say that?" I choked. "I get the feeling I'm being pushed back into the 19th century, legalism and all!"

"I have a better question for you." He was still smiling, which unnerved me. I have never enjoyed discussing strongly differing views with him, because there are so few arguments that I have ever won. Besides, at that time in our marriage I had a long list of his views that I was just waiting to change. I didn't want him on the offensive. He spoke anyway.

"Why are you reacting so strongly?"

I started to say that I wasn't "reacting," but his question made me so angry that I couldn't say it without raising my voice (and flailing my arms and all those other non-reactionary type actions). Besides, we were in public. I smiled sweetly as another couple walked by.

Bill continued. "I think we should at least take his suggestion: pray about it, and try a six-week fast from contemporary Christian music."

All things are lawful for me, but all things are not expedient. All things are lawful for me, but all things do not edify. 1 Corinthians 10:23- 24

"But, I don't agree," I said through frozen smile. "This teaching shackles with dos and don'ts, shoulds and shouldn'ts. It's binding, it's restrictive, it's works-oriented – and it's legalism!"

Bill thought for a long moment, which gave me hope. (It was a great speech!) Finally, he spoke.

"I think this is one area where we're not going to be in agreement. I really think we should do this."

> Character is who we are when our opinions are challenged.

I was livid. "Can you tell me why you are camping on this one particular point? There are so many other things that we've heard this week, so many other places where we could begin working. Why not try starting with something that's on both of our lists?!"

He was unmoved. "Because I see a lot of good fruit. What if he's right?"

Be ye followers of me, even as I also am of Christ. 1 Corinthians 11:1

Bill continued, while I pouted. "I want to see for myself if what he says has merit – if this is as true for me as he says it is for him. Didn't we hear that those who might be addicted to rock music become, let's see, what was that word? Ah, yes…reactionary? Yes, they tend to become defensive and reactionary if you suggest that they remove their music for even a six-week trial."

Inwardly I wanted his head, but I smiled and said nothing.

And I, brethren, could not speak unto you as to spiritual, but as to carnal, even as to babes in Christ. 1 Corinthians 3:1

"Besides," he went on. "If it's really a mixing of the message of the gospel with the music of the world, we don't want to continue raising our children in it, do we?"

But, take heed lest by any means this liberty of yours become a stumbling block to them that are weak. 1 Corinthians 8:9

I had lost. I'd been afraid that I was going to lose through the entire conversation. I could tell he'd already made a decision. My only chance was to be quiet, and hope that he would get busy with work and other activities and forget to follow through.

But, he didn't forget. A week after that fateful conversation our music (my music) was all in storage. I began to show serious signs of withdrawal but Bill was unmoved.

But, when you sin so against the brethren, and wound their weak conscience, you sin against Christ. 1 Corinthians 8:12

That music stayed in storage for three years. We replaced contemporary Christian music (Christian rock) with classical music and life went on. During that time I couldn't have told you if I noticed much difference in our spiritual lives. The children grew, and we still had some friction in our marriage that came and went, friction with the children that came and went, some times of insight and blessings that came and went, and some average times that came and went. Life just went on.

Then one day, while alone in the car, I tuned to a brand-new contemporary Christian station, the first for our area. I will never forget the shock that I received, as I "tasted" that which we had left behind.

Three things hit me very clearly in only a moment. First, I had a strong sense that I was listening to a mixed message. It was somewhat like forcing oil and water to mix. They *can* mix, but only if they're kept moving so rapidly that you can't tell where one ends and the other begins. If you slow them down to analyze them, you see how incompatible they are.

Secondly, I realized that my musical "appetite" had adjusted to the classical music and sweet hymns in our home. Without my even being aware of it, I had evidently become accustomed to the soothing atmosphere they'd been producing. The music that I was listening to in the car had a spirit of independence, of pride, of self, and of the flesh that I had never (ever) been able to recognize before. It seemed quite obvious in that moment that the music opposed Christ-like humility even though its words embraced it.

The Spirit wars with the flesh, and the flesh with the spirit.

Galatians 5:17

Thirdly, the beat was still extremely appealing to me. So, while my heart was moved by the spiritual lyrics, my flesh was pulled by the fleshly music and the beat. It was having these two different parts of myself, which I was suddenly aware were used to working in opposition to each other, now both attracted to the same thing that made it easy to sense what a spiritually dulling effect that it had had on us.

Watch and pray that you enter not into temptation; the spirit indeed is willing, but the flesh is weak. Matthew 26:41

Up to this point, and because of our divided opinions on the issue, we hadn't said anything to the children about music. That night, after listening to my comments, Bill conducted a sort of "laboratory test" with them, then ages 9, 5, 4 and 2. He turned to a popular rock station, played a sound bite, and asked the question, "Does this sound (the music itself) worldly or godly?"

"Worldly!" was the unanimous opinion. Even, Jon, who had lived six years of his life with our Christian rock music, smiled knowingly and admitted, "Worldly."

Bill repeated this experiment down the dial until he reached the Christian contemporary station. He gave it the same sound bite. "Worldly music," came the unanimous vote, with looks of, "Dad, this is easy. Don't you know that?" Bill then turned the Christian station back on and this time asked the children to listen to the words. When our children realized that a spiritual message could be mixed with worldly music,

> Cravings are strong desires for that which we've already tasted and become accustomed to.

they registered surprise and confusion. "How can they do that?" asked our five-year old. Their unadulterated tastes were offended.

Rock music sounds good, feels good and is addictive no matter the lyrics. Addictions tend to blind those who are hooked on them. This kind of addiction is spiritually-discerned. I could not "see" until that night I heard the music after a long absence that musical tastes, just like the taste buds, could be affected by exposure. Cravings are strong desires for that which we've already tasted and become accustomed to. Had we continued to saturate our children with Christian rock (as we had begun with our oldest), they too would have grown accustomed to it, found a place in their hearts for it, and then craved it.

The term "contemporary" means current, modern or present-day. The "current, modern and present-day" music of which a vast amount of contemporary Christian music is modeled is correctly called "rock-and-roll." The softer beat has been rightly labeled, "soft rock." Since contemporary Christian music imitates the world's music, then it's reasonable to expect that it should be called by the more correct name – "Christian rock-and-roll," or "soft Christian rock."

The fact that people have been saved or have experienced positive Spiritual change while listening to Christian rock (as we were) simply affirms the power of a seed of Scriptural truth to bear fruit in men's hearts through nearly any medium or format. It doesn't validate the format. When Paul said that he became "all things to all men in order to save some"[63] he wasn't speaking of partaking in the pleasures of those to whom he was sent in order to win them, but of surrendering his rights to all things that might cause those to whom he was sent to stumble.

Bill and I were both steeped in secular rock-and-roll as teens, and I would be misleading if I didn't confess here and now that when certain songs (and certain types of songs) happen to play I find that I still very much enjoy them, either for their fun beat or warm message. I will also admit that during times of discouragement or frustration or anger that I have secretly slid the radio dial to an old soft rock station looking for comfort, or to assuage my negative feelings. I was searching for some good feeling to chase away the bad ones – fixing feelings with feelings – because I was not yet willing (or yet desperate enough) to cry out to the Lord for help to fix the real problem. But, I've never been tempted to return to the Christian rock station because the mixing of spiritual and worldly doesn't comfort, but grieves me to this day. It's the mixing, the imitation that offends now.

When we go out with our children, whether running errands, doing good works, or serving the needy, we are "in the world." We can't help but hear worldly music. We expect it – and we give, serve, love and work around it and in it and through it. It's part of "being in the world." We don't expect the world to change their standards to match our convictions. Both the words and the music are compatible, and give the same message.

Music is powerful, and has a strong pull. If we've experienced its pull in our own lives, we understand how strong it can be in the lives of our children. If we see areas of independence, pride or rebellion in our children, if our children become reactionary or possessive if asked to consider putting away their music to ask the Lord's direction about it, if they aren't growing spiritually or seem to be drifting away, then it would only be reasonable and prudent for us to put away anything in our own lives that is questionable for the sake of our children.

No one could reasonably argue that the influence of rock-and-roll hasn't damaged our culture. The effects so obviously surround us. But is it only the words that damage? Or can there be something in the music, the repetitive beat, the addiction to it, or the spirit of it that also dulls or damages? Is it possible that the world's music is "rocking" us to a sleep where we only dream of some day surrendering everything to the Lord – everything except our tastes in music? Bill protected our family from potential harm when we didn't know the answers to those questions, even when we weren't in agreement. If our children's character is more important than music, then we will limit our freedoms for the sake of our children – the weaker brethren.

Television

...I will walk within my house with a perfect heart. I will set no wicked thing before my eyes... Ps 101:2-3

From Bill: I grew up in a TV generation. It was our babysitter, our playmate, and our teacher. There was nothing on the air then that was even mildly objectionable by today's standards. Cher's outfits, whatever the Smothers Brothers could get past the network censors and the go-go dancers on Laugh-In were about as bad as I remember. Those were the days of the first runs of Gilligan's Island, The Beverly Hillbillies and Green Acres. The Flintstones came on in prime time and Disney's "wonderful world" was not yet in color. The highlight of my year would be when the new shows started. I would plan my life around which TV shows were on (this was long before the VCR – come to think of it, it was before the audio cassette as well). The greatest punishment I could imagine was to not be allowed to watch my favorite shows (and I had a lot of them). To this day I can still remember my father giving my sister, brother and me the "opportunity" of choosing our own punishment for some offense. I don't remember what I chose (it probably involved some type of physical punishment), but I do remember that my sister chose to be completely restricted from watching TV for a week. That was inconceivable to me. I can still remember the amazement I felt each time I saw her going to bed as the rest of us were watching it.

During high school, the first thing I did was to turn on the TV and watch whatever was on while I was doing my homework (or sometimes instead of my homework). Even after I was married and we had our first child, I can remember coming home from work and spending hours watching shows in the evening, many of them reruns from years earlier. I was addicted to the TV, I knew, but I enjoyed it and had no intention of quitting.

It was during that time that I read a book[64] that spoke to me. I'm not going to try to explain exactly what spoke to me from that book, because that is really not the point of this book. Whatever it was, it was sufficient to convince me that "as for me and my house," we would no longer watch broadcast TV. I remember reading the book while lying in bed. When I finished the section on TV I got up, unplugged the TV, and I think I put it out in the garage. My only point of indecision was whether to throw it away, give it away, or sell it. I was so convicted that I was not sure if it would be morally wrong for me to supply the means for anyone to watch TV. I eventually gave it away.

That night was one of the turning points in my life. It was a conviction that took hold immediately and I have never been tempted to go back. That's not to say that I have not been tempted to watch TV. Remember, I'm a self proclaimed TV addict. I've still been known to "flesh out" in front of the TV when we are on vacation, and I've exposed my children to more old TV shows than is probably good for them. I've even been known to dig out the rabbit ears for something of historical significance (or even an occasional end-of-season game if the Gators are having a good year). But I have never been tempted to go back to having cable or even broadcast TV generally available in our home again. I had no idea that night what a change it would make in our lives, but I do know that we would never have come to the good place we are today unless we were willing to "set no wicked thing before my eyes."

In retrospect, I can see that it was probably the single most important change we made in our home after we were married. It protected our children and us from untold temptations. We were able to separate ourselves from the contemporary culture when the children were all so young and concentrate on the things around us that really mattered.

> That night was one of the turning points in my life.

I think that it's ironic that someone who did most of his growing up in the 60's and 70's where there was such an emphasis on rebelling against authority and "doing your own thing" (of course your own thing had to be just like every other teenager's "own thing"), would grow up to be more conservative than his parents and more of a rebel against contemporary society than he ever was as a youth.

From Mardy: When Bill changed his view of television (pun intended), it was another situation where I didn't share his conviction. Consequently, I went through withdrawal and during times of stress I asked him to put up an antenna for broadcast or to purchase cable, which he never did. As the years went by, we both were subjected to others' opinions that we were being overprotective by sheltering our children from the "real world," and that there was something good to be learned from any program (even if it was only to not follow the star's example).

At the same time, I began to notice a greater difference between the root problems that we had been busy dealing with (many of our own doing), and the disheartening additional media-baggage that other families, whose children had few television restrictions, were facing. I had to admit that our children were never obsessed with super-heroes, did not succumb to clothing or hair fads, rarely pined for whatever new gadgets or toys were being blatantly marketed through kid's TV, and did not pick up any "kids are smarter than adults" attitudes, complete with impatient sighs and rolling of the eyes. When they *were* exposed to those attitudes in children's videos (or in the occasional television program or movie), their opinion was that those children were in serious need of "a trip to the woodshed."

They also missed out on the entire strong mother/weak father, absent parent, single-parent, step-parent, live-in parent, two-career-parent, hypocritical parent and gay parent themes that are so often coupled with confused child, angry child, rebellious child, immoral child, and searching-for-the-right-answer-child scenarios that have been touted as "normal family living" while they were growing up. Instead of feeling restricted, I began to realize that we had been graciously spared. Many years later when we inherited my father's television, Bill allowed family videos on Friday nights with pre-approved movies, usually from a Christian or public library.

A man shows his character by what he laughs at.
German Proverb

The following essay, sent to us by friends, gives a child's-eye-view of compromising standards through television.

A few months before I was born, my dad met a stranger who was new to our small Tennessee town. From the beginning, Dad was fascinated with this enchanting newcomer, and soon invited him to live with our family. The stranger was quickly accepted and was around to welcome me into the world a few months later.

As I grew up I never questioned his place in our family. Mom taught me to love the Word of God. Dad taught me to obey it. But the stranger was our storyteller. He could weave the most fascinating tales. Adventures, mysteries and comedies were daily conversations. He could hold our whole family spellbound for hours each evening. He was like a friend to the whole family. He took Dad and me to our first major league baseball game. He was always encouraging us to see the movies and he even made arrangements to introduce us to several movie stars.

> Our children didn't succumb to fads, rarely pined for toys and didn't pick up any "kids are smarter than adults" attitudes. I began to realize that we'd been graciously spared.

The stranger was an incessant talker. Dad didn't seem to mind, but sometimes Mom would quietly get up while the rest of us were enthralled with one of his stories of faraway places and go to her room read her Bible and pray. I wonder now if she ever prayed that the stranger would leave. You see my dad ruled our household with certain moral convictions. But this stranger never felt an obligation to honor them. Profanity, for example, was not allowed in our house - not from us, from our friends, or adults. Our longtime visitor, however, used occasional four-letter words that burned my ears and made Dad squirm.

To my knowledge the stranger was never confronted. My dad was a teetotaler who didn't permit alcohol in his home, not even for cooking. But the stranger felt we needed exposure and enlightened us to other ways of life. He offered us beer and other alcoholic beverages often. He made cigarettes look tasty, cigars manly, and pipes distinguished. He talked freely (much too freely) about sex. His comments were sometimes blatant, sometimes suggestive, and generally embarrassing. I know now that my early concepts of the man/woman relationship were influenced by the stranger.

As I look back, I believe it was by the grace of God that the stranger did not influence us more. Time after time he opposed the values of my parents. Yet he was seldom rebuked and never asked to leave. More than thirty years have passed since the stranger moved in with the young family on Morningside Drive. But if I were to walk into my parents' den today, you would still see him sitting over in a corner, waiting for someone to listen to him talk and watch him draw his pictures. His name? We always called him TV. Author unknown

Computers and the Internet

*But you, O Daniel, shut up the words, and seal the book,
even to the time of the end (when) many shall run to and
fro, and knowledge shall be increased. Dan 12:4*

High-tech communication adds a new dynamic in regard to protecting our children. The Internet, e-mail, Instant Messaging, chat rooms, cell phones and text-messaging are great communication and research tools – if used by mature people. Having a systems programmer for a dad means that our children use computers – a lot! They have all done typing and math drills, reading, phonics and foreign language programs, online courses, Scripture study and reports on computers. They also email friends and relatives, while the older ones use the Internet. One of our children got his law degree from a distance-learning Christian law school, submitting his assignments online, and engaging in chatroom class discussions. Our children also have their own webpage and e-mail accounts, partly because Bill enjoys keeping us on the cutting edge of technology. However, he let children know when he opened their accounts that he'd retain the right to check them at any time. If a child were giving us reason to check, he would. If they were giving us reason to remove it, he'd do that, too.

> You are the light of
> the world. A city set
> on a hill cannot be
> hidden.
>
> Matthew 5:14

A quick computer quiz:
- Will our children need computer skills for most fields of work or service? Yes.

- Are computers also dangerous? Yes. Can they become addictive? Yes.
- Is the Internet a vast resource of incredible, instant information? Yes.
- Can it become addictive? Yes.
- Is it also filled with dangerous information, with access to dangerous people? Yes.
- Is email a fast, inexpensive and a wonderful communication tool? Yes.
- Can it become addictive? Yes.
- Are there filters available that can keep dangerous information out of our homes? Yes.
- Is there any filter that can keep a smart teen whose heart is not turned toward the Lord out of where he's made up his mind he's going to go? *No!* And our children are getting more computer-savvy by the microsecond.

A computer is a tool, and the Internet a resource. Just like any tool or resource, they can be used to help or to harm, as a time-saver or a time-waster, under control or being controlled by them – depending on the user.

What makes the Internet unique, however, is that the stakes are so high. There is some pretty bad stuff out there, particularly instantly-accessed pornography that is easy to accidentally stumble into even by knowledgeable and mature users.

When we let children (who are less knowledgeable and less mature than adults) or teens (who are more knowledgeable but usually less mature than adults) browse the net with unfiltered Internet access, we set them up to be exposed to harmful and damaging information – whether by accident, curiosity, or intent. With the Internet, the phrase "one picture is worth a thousand words" means that there is no rewind button on our children's minds. Once exposed to adult issues or explicit materials, a certain amount of innocence is lost forever. We then have to operate in the mode of damage-control. Add to that instant exposure to strangers, who can then become online "friends," or even predators, and all of the issues regarding influence are back in play. The Internet's biggest asset is also its most obvious danger: it brings the outside world into the home.

Parents also need to be aware that public libraries generally have unfiltered Internet access. That means that if I can't find a parking spot, and I ask my ten-year old to run inside the library to pick up a book that's being held at the desk, that it's possible for him to see a porn site displayed on a screen by another ten year-old.

> With the Internet, the phrase "one picture is worth a thousand words" means there's no rewind button on our children's minds.

Keeping faith, and a good conscience, which some having put away, have made shipwreck of their faith. 1 Timothy 1:19

An Internet filter obviously can keep out some dangers, but the most effective filter in existence is a clear conscience. Our children's conscience is the 24-hour filter of the heart that goes with them wherever they go (or wherever their mouse may go). Our children will most assuredly be exposed to wrong activities (if not on the Internet, then just outside our doors). We want to teach them to keep a clear conscience by governing themselves and judging their own hearts. They may be tempted and they may even fall, but a tender and clear conscience will be the most effective driving force to get them back up again.

Teenage boys seem to be gravitating like magnets toward computers and the Internet. There's nothing wrong in that pull, per se, as long as the pull doesn't become a drive, and as long as we are aware that the lure for fast, crunchable information brings with it certain risks. If a teen is spending significantly more of his spare time in front of a monitor than with people, or if the majority of his relationships are maintained through a keyboard, that creates an environment for potential problems. If he becomes secretive when asked about his activities, or defensive or reactionary when it's suggested that his computer use be limited, if his computer (or computer-time) becomes more important than his conscience or his relationships with family and friends, if he already displays a weak conscience in other areas – then he isn't yet mature enough or self-governing enough to be using so powerful (and risky) a tool.

Incredibly, limiting computer use can be even tougher to do than removing friends! While friends can represent identity and fellowship and approval, computers also represent independence, knowledge, power and control. Parents who believe that their teen is already addicted or getting to sites he or she shouldn't be accessing need to really cry out to the Lord for their teen's heart. Removing the computer won't cause that child to change any more than removing wrong friends or music will cause him to build strong character. But exposing our children to people or media or tools that can have strong influence (and strong effect) before they are mature enough to govern themselves brings potential long-term damage. Only God can change the heart, and we must cry out to the Lord for our children's hearts.

Computer Games and Video Games

If I wanted to design a way to divert people from making an impact in the world, I would create another world – where every decision that was made and every effort expended had no effect on real life at all.

That statement was made by one of our teens late one Friday night after he'd spent more time than he felt he should have playing a "cool" new computer game he'd just purchased with birthday money. I glanced up at him from my bed where I had been cozily working on this book for most of the evening. I wanted to give his incredible insight the consideration and feedback it so rightly deserved, but I couldn't. My thoughts were suddenly consumed with finding a subtle way to minimize the *FreeCell* game (my own computer-game weakness of which I had just won my fourth round) before his eye caught the reflection of my screen in a mirror.

Computer games and video games are fast becoming the standard of sophisticated play. While relaxation and downtime are important for children (and adults), electronic games pose the same type of exposure and addiction pitfalls that Internet use does.

Our own children have played their share of computer games, generally on Friday nights. We don't want young children to spend the majority of their free time playing computer games rather than interacting with others. Physical play not only carries the health benefit of exercise, it's bound by the reality of cause and effect – when you get hit, it really hurts! After a reasonable time, players of a physical game (or even board games) usually tire out and quit, while electronic games tend to become more addictive with time. Children and teens (okay, moms as well) need to have a certain level of internal discipline to keep any game from developing into a habitual time-waster.

A Word about Standards

If when exposed to truth we see that our standards (behaviors, rules of living) change, we need to be careful that we don't judge others whose standards (behaviors, rules of living) have not changed, or are different than ours. The freedom gained through living our convictions is minimal compared to the bondage incurred through judging others! Standards are supposed to be the outward expression of inward beliefs. We can only live our inward beliefs by God's grace anyway, so we have nothing to boast about.

Our duty as *Christians* is to judge ourselves, but our duty as *parents* is to protect our children. We removed ourselves and our children from exposure to Christian rock music in fellowship and in worship because of that responsibility to protect them. Removing ourselves from that environment without judging our brothers and sisters who remain in it gives us credibility when teaching our children how to stand for their own convictions without an attitude of judgment. Again, we don't expect our family, friends or a church to change *their* standards because of *our* beliefs.

For if we would judge ourselves, we should not be judged.
I Corinthians 11:31

While we have had to explain to family, friends and church members our beliefs about friends, music, television and other influences (particularly as they pertained to our children's participation, or nonparticipation, in an event), we don't discuss (i.e.: preach) our beliefs about them unless we're asked. It's not our duty to promote our beliefs about our rules for living to those who don't ask, or to try to convince those who don't have our beliefs to adopt our standards. We've never met anyone who, having been strongly affected by issues such as contemporary Christian music or television (as we were), became convinced to give them up simply by listening to someone else tell them that they should. Even for Bill, who gave someone the benefit of the doubt, music had to be spiritually discerned, and then only after a long period of time away from it.

Visiting in relatives' homes can pose a challenge, especially if our relatives don't understand our convictions (or they understand, but don't agree), if our children's cousins have unmonitored access to television, computer games or music, or if a television or computer stays turned on throughout a visit. Our children may also be tempted to test whose authority they're under while in relatives' homes, even if they haven't been testing rules at home. In addition, there may be books or magazines (or even graphic newspaper pictures or articles) that we don't want young children to see. We need to protect our children from negative media-exposure without judging relatives who don't have the same conviction. Even if we have the right attitude (which I have failed at many times), it's still no guarantee that we won't be misunderstood or seen as legalistic or judgmental, or that our children won't feel isolated at a family gathering, or feel uninformed about a popular movie or a current trend or a graphic event in the news.

All of these potentially uncomfortable situations can actually be wonderful training opportunities for practicing the true purpose of socialization – teaching our children (while under our wing where we can observe their progress) how to socialize with (and love) those whose convictions are different from their own (as opposed to sending them out unsupervised for long periods with those whose convictions are different, and hoping that they will maintain our standards before they have even developed convictions of their own). We want our children to eventually become self-governing in the midst of strong influence, so we begin by training them in character in the extended family, the neighborhood, the church and the world. It's training them as we "walk by the way."

However, if the influence is too strong, if our children are not mature enough to stand, if the consequences for failure would be too great, then we gently pull them back under our wing – sometimes to retrain, sometimes to wait until they mature a little more.

A child doesn't realize how important his character is or how valuable his soul is, and he can easily be tempted to trade them for approval or temporal pleasure.

How our children respond to influences in the family, the church, or the world depends a great deal, not on the influencer, but on them – on their own character. Woe unto us, if while their character is still being formed we put stumbling blocks of negative influence in front of them that can cause them to stumble. A child doesn't realize how important his character is or how valuable his soul is, and he can easily be tempted to trade them for approval or temporal pleasure. Training our children while under our wing how to love and accept those whose standards are different builds character. Sending them out alone to spend time with people or activities that contradict or ignore our training (for the purpose of approval, socialization, entertainment or pleasure) erodes character. We want to guard who or what influences our children. We are the ones who are supposed to have their best interest at heart. Let us surround young children with those people and things which promote godliness.

Chapter Ten: Traps on the Path to Character
Legalism, Pride and Discouragement

There are plenty of traps waiting to ensnare on the path to raising our children. If we learn to recognize and avoid them, we save ourselves (and our children) untold trials. If we recognize that we're already in any of these traps, we want to become free (and help to set our children free). We also want to avoid passing our own "trap-weaknesses" to our children.

The Trap of Legalism

Legalism happens when a parent (or a family, or an individual, or a church) places more value on standards and rules than on people. Just like Pharisees, we can know a lot and have strong opinions about what we know, and then fall into the delusion that what we know is important than loving people.

Understanding Principles, Standards and Rules

Principles are truths (or "facts of life") that don't change. Principles affect us whether we believe them or reject them, understand them or forget them. It behooves man to understand God's principles.[65] Our acceptance of the *principle* of gravity, for example, causes us to adopt *standards* of behavior that keep us from jumping out of tall windows. If a person doesn't know about the principle of gravity (such as a toddler), his lack of understanding can result in unwise standards (such as playing near open windows). He requires *rules*[66] (or laws) placed on him to keep him from going near open windows for his own protection. If he breaks those rules, the principle remains true and in effect – whether he ever falls out of a window or not.

We want to teach our children about principles (which don't change), while enforcing rules (which may change) until they develop their own convictions about those principles. If our children sense that they are more important to us than the rules that they keep or break, they will more easily transition into adopting their own right standards of behavior.

Standards (of behavior) result from decisions that we make based on our own individual convictions about a truth or principle. Every person (every family, every church and every group) has particular standards of behavior that vary (either slightly or greatly) from those around them. Spoken or unspoken, thought out or assumed, they define what the acceptable standards are within that unit. In the family, those standards can be seen in areas such as etiquette and manners, music and entertainment, money and investments, dating, courtship, dress, family planning, worship and more.

> Legalism happens when an individual, a family, or a church places more value on standards and rules than on people.

As our children begin to develop standards based on their own convictions, it's important to teach them how dangerous it is to judge others by how they fulfill (or don't fulfill) certain standards.[67] Standards don't guarantee character (as with the Pharisees). Standards are supposed to reflect inner convictions.[68] We want our children to draw others to truth (not to standards), so that they can impart truth (and not standards) to them. Otherwise they run the risk of mistaking high standards as strong character.

They also need to understand that their own standards can only be kept through the power of the cross. If they judge others for not living up to their standards, or cling to their own standards without depending on the Lord to help them to fulfill them, they will also fall into legalism. If they see us treat others as more valuable than the standards that they break or fulfill, they will learn how to view and treat others as more valuable than the standards that others break or fulfill.

Rules (or laws) are designed to force compliance to a standard when we cannot (or will not, or do not know how to) live by principle. The Ten Commandments were *"Ten Rules"* God placed on rebellious Israel to point them toward a standard of behavior that was really only achievable through the coming Christ. They were rules that were *never* placed on their father Abraham whose standard of behavior was dictated by (the *principle* of) faith. In the Sermon on the Mount Jesus introduced a higher *standard* of behavior than Abraham or the Law because he revealed a greater *principle*[69] *(*the Truth became flesh).[70] That's why He took the Pharisees to task when they judged the disciples (who were learning to live by the principle of faith) for grabbing a drive-through ear of corn as they traveled with Him. The Pharisees were like rebellious tattletales complaining that other children were breaking the rules. They just didn't realize they were tattling to the very Parent who had created the rule, and that as long as He walked with them, they were in no danger of falling.

Until our children develop right standards of their own, we rightly establish rules for them. However, because of the loosened moral standards today, parents are tempted to react by swinging too far in the direction of rules and control. If we create rules in reaction to society (instead of conviction based on principle), the result will be legalism. If we enforce rules based on family tradition, personal reputation, church policy, social status or other non-essential matters (instead of principles), that, too, can result in legalism. Our children may then feel shackled by those rules (especially as teens when their convictions about truth begin to take hold), and begin to chafe against them. If we tighten those rules in response to their pulling against them, they may break away from us altogether (emotionally or physically). When that happens, they sometimes carelessly throw off even foundational rules that were once easy to handle.

Even the compliant teen who somehow manages to humble himself under fearful, reactionary, overbearing, overprotective or controlling parents will eventually sense that those rules, once fences of protection from the dangers of the world, were erected in fear, and have become walls of potential division between parent and child. It would take a mature teen, indeed, to receive more grace and insight than his parents and to allow God to use such restriction to conform him to the image of Christ.

If our children's keeping of rules becomes more important to us than they are, then we are trapping them in legalism. To paraphrase Mark,[71] *The standard was made for the child (for his benefit, well-being and good), not the child for the standard.*

As our children get closer to maturity, they'll assuredly develop some convictions that are different from our own. Ours certainly have. We need to grant them the freedom of that difference. We may rightfully require that they keep our rules as children, but we can't insist that they adopt our convictions as adults. It's a good idea to reexamine our convictions in light of theirs. Though I have been pulled from various traps numerous times by Bill (and by others), it has been a new experience to be pulled from legalism by a child's convictions that showed me that I had been clinging to rules.

As our children grow into adults, they will begin to relate to us more as brothers and sisters in Christ (which indeed they are), instead of simply as sons and daughters over whom we are stewards for a short season.

The Trap of Pride

...He (Nebuchadnezzar) walked in the palace of the kingdom of Babylon. The king spoke, and said, "Is not this great Babylon, that I have built for the house of the kingdom by the might of my power, and for the honor of my majesty?"
Daniel 4:28-30

Now it came to pass that as I was walking about our church grounds one evening after a service, yea, that a friend did approach me and said unto me, "The conflicts in my life are not of my own doing. Yea, I am innocent, and the problems in my life lay with my husband, children, and furthermore with all those who are around me."

Immediately this friend's manifold blind spots and faults came before my mind, and I pondered them within my heart, saying, "Yea, if only she were as spiritual as I, she would see that her own pride hath made her blind to her own faults."

I then strolled about the church grounds reflecting within my mind upon my own life saying, "Are these children that we have, and their fine character, not proof that we have chosen God's ways? Did not we ourselves build this character into them, through principles which we ourselves did humbly apply, and nay, we did neither make whiny excuses, nor pout, nor blame, but faithfully followed only in His truths?"

And I did condescend unto her, and made manifold judgments about her in my heart, and I did not pity her plight, which I saw that she herself had made with her own hands.

While the word was in the king's mouth, there fell a voice from heaven, saying, "O king Nebuchadnezzar, to you it is spoken, "The kingdom is taken from you. And they shall drive you from men, and your dwelling shall be with the beasts of the field. They shall make you eat grass like an ox, and seven times shall pass over you, until thou know that the most High rules in the kingdom of men, and gives it to whomsoever he will." Daniel 4:31-32

Immediately thereafter, a strong thought came unto me. "Let us sell our nice home in the city and let us move into a hundred year-old broken down house away from the city (for half the price of our current home)." And my husband, whose heart had been turned toward debt-free living, agreed therein, saying, "Yes, and Amen."

Thus, we were driven away from friends, and our dwelling place became with no heat or air conditioning, yea, even with no cabinets or cupboards, with no friends nearby, with no ministry, nay, not even with phone ringing or visitors coming. And thereafter did few seek us out for fellowship, nay, not even one for counsel.

And I did walk about in the heat crying day and night, "O Lord, Maker of all that is pleasant, deliver Thou us, who are your choice and great servants, from this hot place."

And when the summer sun did relent and the winter winds did blow, I did shiver about in the cold, crying, "Boo-hoo, boo-hoo." And I did crave and whine for leeks and onions.[72] And my husband did say unto me, "Dearest, thou hast grown claws and fangs."

And at the end of the days, I Nebuchadnezzar lifted up my eyes unto heaven, and my understanding returned to me, and I blessed the most High, and I praised and honored him that lives forever, whose dominion is an everlasting dominion, and His kingdom is from generation to generation. And all the inhabitants of the earth are reputed as nothing and He does according to his will in the army of heaven, and among the inhabitants of the earth, and none can stay his hand, or say unto him, "What are you doing?" Daniel 4:34-35

And many summers and winters passed over us, until mine eyes were opened unto the state of mine own heart. Thus did mine own pride become apparent unto me and lo, it did stink and was repulsive unto me, and did cause me great anguish of soul. And I did walk about in mine anguish crying day and night, "Oh Lord, Maker of all that is good, do remove the pride from this uplifted heart! Deliver Thou me from my iniquity and vanity of heart!"

At the same time my reason returned to me, and for the glory of my kingdom, mine honor and brightness returned to me, and my counselors and my lords sought me, and I was established in my kingdom, and excellent majesty was added to me. Now I Nebuchadnezzar praise and extol and honor the King of heaven, all whose works are truth, and his ways judgment, and those that walk in pride He is able to abase. Daniel 4:36-37

And verily, verily, He gaveth unto me a new understanding, and He removed the haughty look and the condescending way. And I did give thanks for His blessings, and His truths and His mercies, which were from His hand, as well as His forgiveness and His grace wherein we did partake. And I did gain insight and understanding that it is God Almighty who is able to humble and to make great, and to build character, and that it by His mercy that we stand or fall, and not by any wisdom or power that we ourselves possess.[73]

Pride

Comparing themselves with themselves they became unwise...[74]

Another common trap on the path to character is pride, and it can come through comparison. Pride blinds us to our own shortcomings, makes us immune to correction, isolates us from fellowship, cuts us off from God's grace, justifies our feelings – and passes to the next generation.

Most of the time we're not even aware that we have it unless we find ourselves either overreacting to others (including our own children), or see that we are "over-impressed" with ourselves (or our own children). If we are more excited about our children's performance (or trophy, or status, or grade) than they are, if we think that they are better than others, or that they are special and will not fall, or that they are too smart to be fooled, or that they deserve better or more or nicer – then we've already fallen into the trap of pride.

Pride encourages us to justify ourselves, and once we succumb to it, makes us feel better about ourselves. It's like an illegal drug: it feels good while it slowly kills us. It's the hardest trap to recognize because it truly blinds us to our own faults, while magnifying others'.

... be clothed with humility, for God resists the proud, but gives grace to the humble. I Peter 5:5

The only cure for pride is humility. And humility can't be mentally assented-to (or assigned); it has to be put on. The first time I clothed myself with true humility to ask forgiveness from several people was scary. Humility eventually involves people, and usually people who know us quite well (like our families). The more pride we have, the less spiritual those to whom we must humble ourselves seem. Even though there was great joy (and relief) in following through, I immediately slipped out of that unusual feeling of humility, and back into my comfort zone of independence and pride.

Pride can be very easy (or nearly impossible) to recognize in our children because it can cause us to either overreact to their pride – or become blind to it. Unless we truly humble ourselves (and cry out to the Lord for help), we will be unable to recognize our own pride – and unable to help our children recognize theirs. As we humble ourselves we teach our children by example how to humble themselves.

> As we humble ourselves we teach our children by example how to humble themselves.

In addition, if we praise children for accomplishments or talents or natural beauty, they are more susceptible to falling into the trap of pride. But, if we are overly-critical toward them, they can fall into the trap of pride in their search for self-worth. As we praise our children for genuine character, and begin to clothe ourselves with humility, we show our children how to clothe themselves with humility, and avoid the blinding trap of pride.

Discouragement from Comparison to Others

While pride fills us with false confidence, discouragement paralyzes us with hopeless feelings and can plague us with negative thoughts that seem to be more true than others' counsel or even Scripture. Like pride, discouragement can also come from comparison. Sometimes it comes from comparing a new standard with the reality of where we, or our family, are now. It can come from comparing ourselves with other parents, or our children with other children, or from comparing the progress of one child with that of another, or from comparing our own potential to our actual progress.

Shortly after I understood the concept of accepting myself as I was, I attended a seminar in which I spent four and one-half days at the feet of incredibly successful moms with incredibly character-filled children, who offered many incredible insights and testimonies. The only problem was that by the time I arrived at the conference I was discouraged and depressed. I had just driven 600 miles with five children who had trashed the van and fought over everything, including who had a window seat. We had even broken down on the road and arrived late. I had turned into a Momzilla before we had finished unpacking. Instead of receiving encouragement that week, I could only focus on how "far behind" we were compared to everyone else.

As I wandered into the large auditorium for yet another depressing comparison-session disguised as encouragement, I slipped to the very top row of the very top section, so that the speaker became a tiny speck far below. I told myself that it was for her own good that I sat so far away: if I were any closer I would probably throw a character booklet at her.

As I sat there, focusing on the speck that was taking me on yet another lap around the Comparison Track, dark thoughts encompassed me like black clouds, and before long they began raining on me. I sighed with painful resignation and bitterness, and said in my heart:

I give up. I will never – ever – get to where that mom is. I will never be as together, or as spiritual as that woman.

And as soon as I thought it, another thought came to mind.

You are right. You never will.

But, there was no condemnation, no judgment, no fear in that thought. Only sweet, liberating truth that seemed to be cutting away the darkness and setting me free.

As I thought about those words, and focused on that speck of a speaker, I realized that the physical distance that I had placed between us was very similar to the distance that I felt between where she was spiritually compared to where I was: almost too far to focus on. I would never be able to catch up to her. Then another thought came gently to my mind.

You do not know where she began.

Again that gentle rebuke. I suddenly became aware of the great distance that God had brought me thus far. As though glancing over my own shoulder, I was able to take in the many things in my past that He had already changed. There were sins from my past from which our children had now been protected. I realized that where I could have been, where our family *should* have been without God's mercy, was a long (long) way back, and where I was at that moment was much further than I had ever dreamed I would one day be. It had only been by His grace that we had come this far. In that moment, I was able to accept that I had my own starting point, and my own pace, that there would always be those ahead (many of whom I would never "catch up to"), those alongside (whom I could walk with), and those coming from behind (that I might be able to encourage). That lady on the stage probably began her journey with the Lord many miles ahead of where I was even now, or where I would ever be.

I had been right. I would never get to where she was, because God wanted me to accept where I was.

And thus, my next lesson: once we accept *who* we really are, we need to accept *where* we really are – and that we may not always be where we really want to be, or where we really think we should be. I had accepted my *failures* and put them into His hand; I needed to accept my *progress* (as well as my own inexperience and immaturity) and leave it in His hand.

I wish I could say that I learned my lesson from that experience, but I have fallen into the trap of discouragement numerous times since then. Comparison is so dangerous because it can blind us with pride or beat us down with discouragement. The comparing that God wants us to do is between Him and ourselves, between His word and our lives. As we see the difference, we recognize our need, and cry out to Him to save us – even from ourselves.

Discouragement from Comparison to an Ideal

Martha, Martha. Mary has chosen the better part, and it shall not be taken away from her.[75]

Discouragement can also come from trying to fulfill an ideal. Ideals are beliefs about the way something should be. They usually carry high expectations. Sometimes we need to lower our expectations in regard to ourselves and others.

One afternoon Bill found me in the back yard clipping hedges to vent frustration. I felt like I was suffocating from all of my trials, and I was in a foul mood. Since I knew that Bill knew I was stressed, I assumed that he would be open to my idea that we all get away to see my mom (1000 miles away). But, when I mentioned it (with big, sharp hedge clippers in hand) he said that he did not think that we had the funds for such a trip. I didn't want to think about whether he was right; I wanted to escape.

"Let's go anyway, and pay for it when we get back," I tried.

"Let's pray for the Lord to show us if He wants us to go by providing the money before we leave," he countered.

I somehow knew that God wouldn't be interested in funding any of my "trial-escape plans." So I did what other famous men and women in the Bible did when they were confronted with truth: I tried to stone the messenger. I threw the hedge clippers (to the ground, not at Bill) and told him that I simply had to go.

He looked at me with surprise and asked me teasingly, "Say, you don't suppose the Lord wants you learn a little more *character*, do you?"

At that remark, I started jumping up and down on the hedge clippers, yelling at the top of my lungs, "I AM SICK TO DEATH OF HEARING ABOUT CHARACTER! ALL I WANT TO DO IS GO AWAY! AND I NEVER WANT TO HEAR ABOUT CHARACTER FOR THE REST OF MY LIFE!"

> Comparison is so dangerous because it can blind us with pride or beat us down with discouragement.

I folded my arms and waited for Bill to respond. But true to his dry, phlegmatic sense of humor, he only lifted his eyebrows and looked at me over his glasses as though he were an underpaid psychiatrist and I his simple-minded patient.

What I was actually suffering from was a case of my own expectations of how I thought my life *should* be. Even though it was not reasonable to have very high expectations with six children in the house (three of whom were preschoolers), I had unrealistic ideals about how the house should look, how the children should dress, how nutritious and tasty our meals should be, how our school day should go, how the children should respond, how the house should be fixed, and generally what my life should be like. I was not where I had imagined myself to be ten or twenty years before. Many expectations were unfulfilled, many standards had plummeted, and worse, in reaction to my plight, I was not who I had always thought that I really was. That was scary.

Stress is the difference between where we think we are supposed to be – and reality.

In the months that followed, being pressed by circumstances from which I couldn't escape or change, I cried out to the Lord for help. That help came in the form of grace to accept the fact that my ideas about what I thought my life should be like were not very close to reality. I had accepted my failures and who I really was, and was learning to accept where I really was in my spiritual walk; now I had to adapt my expectations to the reality of my environment.

That meant that certain ideals had to go. The house stayed messier than I liked, but I was able to look past the messes a little easier. Meal planning became simpler as I yielded to Bill's conviction that all foods are blessed if we thank God for them, and ask Him to bless them.[76] Faces were a little dirtier, shoes went untied a little more, clothes or socks didn't always match, and sometimes I slept in or let the children sleep in. I paled in comparison to the Proverbs 31 excellent wife who rose early, stayed up late and did profitable work all day long. My expectations had plummeted.

But our family had a little more time for each other. We played a few more games, traveled a little more, and as the children grew traveled a lot more, laughed a little more and enjoyed each other more. I had replaced the Proverbs 31 wife with Mary of Luke 10, who didn't let pressing needs of the moment (even an important dinner guest) keep her from sitting at Jesus' feet. She chose preparation of her heart over preparation for dinner – and the better part, Jesus had said, would not be taken away from her.

Discouragement from Disorder

Disorder is isn't just untied shoelaces and an occasional dirty face as we dash out the door. It's missing shoes again when we're late, and dirty faces because we spent the hour before departure in search of matching clothes, missing library books – and *my* purse. Clutter may be necessary, yea, even character-building – but disorder is discouraging.

Our children are older now and order is no longer a major issue. There are many practical things a family can do to try to keep order. The most effective organizational systems usually eliminate extra steps (handle it once or toss it out), delegate duties among family members (we shifted some responsibility for record-keeping and filing to the children), and have a centrally-located place for everything.

Here are some things we did when we had a house full of elementary and middle school age children. A 2-drawer filing cabinet (easy for children to access) filled with color-coded folders (each student had his own color) made keeping track of paperwork easier. The children had to put their work (finished or unfinished) into their own folders at the end of the day. We also had our children grade most of their own papers (under a watchful eye if necessary).

Delegating household chores as part of the daily school schedule was another way to we tried to keep order, and it is good character training for children. Three year-olds can help with kitchen chores, five year-olds can load the dishwasher, eight year-olds can wash their own laundry and strip and remake their own beds. It's true that it takes more time and effort to properly train children the first few times, but, it pays for itself in saved time later, and in the reward of more responsible children.

We delegated a lot of their schoolwork as well. At the beginning of the week each child received their school work and chores list. They were to complete them by Friday. Copying spelling words, reading five hours of literature from a pre-selected bookshelf, exercising three days a week, practicing music and computer math drills daily became their responsibility to initiate and complete. If help was needed to understand an assignment, they knew they could ask me. If I wasn't available, they were supposed to advance to something else on their list until I could help them. If I was in a lesson with someone else, they usually figured it out on their own or asked an older sibling. Weekly tasks like weeding a garden or cleaning the fridge also appeared on their lists.

> Our ideals and expectations, our deepest hopes and desires are easy targets for discouragement.

One key to successful delegation is letting children have as much freedom as possible in completing their tasks. We had a couple of go-getters (everything done ahead of schedule), and a couple of more laid-back types. It didn't generally matter to us if all the math assignments were finished on Monday and all the literature read on Tuesday, or if math was done first each day and music later (unless of course the piano had to be played at a certain time). As long as their work was finished by the end of the week (and initialed by mom or dad) it was a "pass." For us, that means joining the rest of the family in popcorn and videos or games on Friday nights. The first time Bill made one of the children finish their assignments while the rest of us had fun, I felt terrible – until that child began to finish his assignments in time! He could have gotten them done, but had chosen not to. Having a list and attaching appropriate consequences helped them to learn responsibility, and cut down on my nagging.

To help keep discouragement at bay, we tried to keep school as simple as possible. If a computer program hit the market that could teach math facts or phonics and spelling, we used it. I knew I needed to save me energies for working on hearts, relationships and life skills as much as possible, things a computer program couldn't do. We also met with other like-minded families for encouragement, tried to keep a weekly date night, and usually got away for a weekend without the children once a year.

What we are doing is very important! We are easy targets for discouragement. The first thing to do when we realize we're being lured away from truth or have fallen into a trap is to call on the Lord. If we will call on Him, He will hear. He longs to be our help in time of trouble. In all of the scenarios I've written about, asking God for help should have been at the top of the list. Many times I let pride or discouragement keep me from crying out for help. It's the most obvious – and the most powerful – tool that we have for every need. In every trial, in every trap, He's waiting to help.

Let's humble ourselves and cry out to the Lord for our children and for ourselves. How much we need Him as parents and how much He delights in helping us when we cry out to Him.

Conclusion

Home education was not the answer to our family's need for strong character. Keeping our children at home and under my wing only helped them to become more like me, consequently emphasizing my own need for change.

True character requires becoming more like Christ, and is the essence of Romans 8:28-29, where a seasoned and tried-in-the-fire apostle explains that being conformed to the image of Christ in all things is our goal. It's something we all want for our children, but discover that in God's requirements for accredited teachers, it's impossible to impart that which we haven't learned.

Home is the campus where a curriculum of Scriptural truths can be lived out by the only teachers who love their students more than they love themselves. Let us cry out to God for grace to raise children of character.

I will open my mouth in a parable. I will utter dark sayings of old which we have heard and known, and our fathers have told us. We will not hide them from their children, showing to the generation to come the praises of the LORD, and His strength, and His wonderful works that He has done. For He established a testimony in Jacob, and appointed a law in Israel which He commanded our fathers that they should make them known to their children, that the generation to come might know them, even the children which should be born, who should arise and declare them to their children that they might set their hope in God, and not forget the works of God, <u>but keep his commandments</u>. Psalm 78:2-7

And what are His commandments we are to teach our children to keep?

Jesus said… "You shall love the Lord you God with all your heart, and with all your soul, and with all your mind. <u>This is the first and great commandment</u>. And the second is like it: you shall <u>love your neighbor as yourself</u>. On these two commandments hang all the Law and the Prophets." Matt 22:37-40

<u>I give you a new commandment, that you love one another</u>. As I have loved you, you should also love one another. By this all shall know that you are My disciples, if you have love for one another. John 13:33-35

From the Authors

From Bill: Much of what you have read in this book is a direct result of Mardy's efforts. Most of my efforts were in setting policy and "putting out fires." I'm a terrible administrator and if weren't for Mardy's amazing gifts in that area we never would have survived. We mostly had the same vision over the years and I've got to give her credit: she usually deferred to my wishes if it came to an impasse. Often I'd come up with some crazy idea and she would have to try to make it work, or convince me that it really was impossible. Since we homeschool our children, Mardy has spent a lot more time with our children than I have.

From Mardy: There is a plethora of books and videos on the market today that give instruction on conflict resolution skills and interpersonal relationships, problem-solving and parenting – even on how to win our children's hearts. But many of them teach us how to look inside ourselves for the answers to our problems, based on our own goodness, wisdom and strength.

> When we become dependent on the Lord, we *show* our children how to become dependent upon Him, rather than *tell* them they should be.

The problem with this type of philosophy is that it usually works to some extent because it's partially true. We *are* made in God's image, and He *has* equipped man with great inner resources, some of which survived the fall – whether man recognizes those gifts as from Him or not.

But God wants us to become like little children, depending on Him for our daily needs whether those needs are for bread or forgiveness or guidance. As He taught us to pray *(Give us this day or daily bread...)* so He wants us to live. When we become dependent upon Him, we can then *show* our children how to become dependent upon Him, rather than *tell* them they should be. We'll never be able to pass on eternal truths using man's wisdom.

If you weren't raised in a nurturing family, as I wasn't, you may have already made a great deal of mistakes and find yourself surrounded by problems staring back at you like little mirrors of yourself. This is where I have found myself many, many (many!) times in the past, experienced again while working on this manuscript, and I know I will face again tomorrow. There are still times I don't first call on the Lord, don't listen before I judge, and don't seek to understand before I speak. Our children still sometimes sin, sometimes break rules and sometimes forget their chores. There are standards that our family (and each member) has adopted and still "forgets," rules that we still disregard or break, and ongoing stupid decisions that we regret. This book is not intended to be about us; we aren't super-Christians who have suddenly arrived. It's about the truths that we've learned. We reap the same good fruit as anyone who applies these truths, and we suffer the same conflicts and consequences as everyone who does not. But, we get up and try again. This book is about the lessons we've learned thus far. It's about God's truths that are super-natural.

Quick-Reference Notes
Ways to Strengthen our Children's Character

- Accept that each crisis, confrontation, challenge, trial we face is a lesson in character on display for our children. View each one as a chance to grow personally, and to demonstrate the kind of choices we also want them to make.
- Follow through on Dad's direction for boundaries and consequences for them, without negative emotion (firm, consistent boundaries w/soft attitudes).
- Choose friends for them when they're young and not yet mature enough to make wise choices.
- Expose them regularly to people whose needs are greater than their own by replacing some or all extra-curricular activities with family ministry: nursing homes~household/yard chores for seniors~taking food to low-income seniors~Ronald McDonald House~helping physically handicapped children, etc.
- As they mature, consider missions trips where they will be pushed out of their comfort zone and must rely on the Lord in a more personal, real way.
- Ask the Lord for at least one positive, same-gender Christian friend for older children, and make times for them to regularly serve somewhere together.
- Allow solid ministries to help train/strengthen older children before leaving home. summit.org/worldviewweeekend.com/worldviewtraining.com, etc

Acknowledgements

Apart from Me, you can do nothing. John 15:5

I am painfully aware of the consequences of working (even on good works) apart from the direction, insight and grace of the Lord Jesus. So it's with deep gratefulness that I must acknowledge the Lord's hand, from beginning to end, on this project. I'm also thankful for the gift of writing with which He has given me, and for the opportunity to use it to help others.

Though I have written much of this book from my own mistakes and perspective, it's truly by both Bill and me. Not only has he patiently carried me, sometimes "kicking and screaming," over to his convictions, but he has carefully helped me with every chapter. I'm deeply grateful for his encouragement, support, editing, insight, patience and love.

For the sweet spirit of support, occasional breakfasts in bed, meals that were cooked while I typed, personal stories I've been allowed to share, and for the fodder for most all of my material, I'm indebted to our children: Jonathan, James, Kate, Daniel, Stephen, Patrick and Joel. For Jonathan's astute job of editing, especially the thought-provoking late-night exchanges, even though they sometimes meant later-night rewrites, I'm very grateful.

For continually encouraging me, especially through my busiest years, to "write that down, Honey, so other moms can hear it," I'm grateful to my mom, Mary.

We're also indebted to Dr. Byron and Faith French, our children's godparents, for the "writer's room" where I could hibernate from time to time, for all the meticulous editing, for providing care for our children so many times when it was needed (and so many times when it wasn't, but you gave of yourselves anyway), for listening so often to our triumphs, for always rooting for truth in the midst of our trials, and for loving us (and our children) exactly as we are.

Many thanks to Genny Busjahn and Dee Privette for their special friendships, and for taking so much time out of their busy days with large families of their own to proofread the manuscript for grammar, readability, and truth.

We're especially grateful to Kathy Sellers, our children's evaluator since 1989, for allowing us to keep our children's character foremost, for encouraging me when I needed it most, and for always praising our children's character development more than their academic progress.

Thank you to Charles Winge (and Carlyn, who is now in Heaven) for all of the patient counsel while we were in the thick of these lessons, and to Ken and Debbi Kennedy, for so graciously letting us "hang out" with your children when they were preteens and young teens, and I needed assurance that there was hope in those busy days of so many little ones, so many demands, and so little insight.

Many thanks to the Florida Parent Educator's Association – particularly Merlinda Hobbs, past Leader's Forum Chair, for the invitation to speak on character to state leadership, Sandra Smith, *Almanac* Editor, for a character column in the *Almanac,* and Muffy Amico, Convention Coordinator, for trusting me with my first workshop at a state convention. And to all of the Florida Homeschooling Leaders who have allowed me the privilege of speaking on character to their groups – Glenn and Cindy, Daniel and Patty, Kerry, Lise, Teresa, Cris, Lori, Rosemarie, Pamela, Robin, Barb, Debbie, Lily, Dee and Joni. It was the preparation for all of those talks that birthed this book.

A very special personal thanks to the moms in my character-focused Moms' Group: Judy, Marilyn, Susan, Genny, Teri, Verna, Barb, Sheri, Lynn, Lee, Polly, Hjorids, Kristy, Ivette,

Acknowledgements

Belinda, Dee Dee, Patricia, Christine, Marilyn, Julie, Lisa, Angie, Lillian, Susan, Linda and Ramona. And to our support group leadership who have attended: Lise, Lisa, Ellen, Bonnie, Wanda, Susan, Juli, Chandra, Debra and Susan. Susan, thank you especially for your gracious hospitality in hosting our meetings. You have all allowed me to flesh out the chapters of this book through our meetings as you listened, shared, bounced off ,added to and encouraged me with your experiences and ideas. I love you all.

~Finally, a super grateful thank you to the friends who answered the call for last-minute, crunch-time edits to the 2007 editions of this book: Patti Ballard, Nikol Hayden, Stephanie Johns, Denise Middleton, Carole Palmer, Moira Rusu and Jennifer Walley. Without your help we'd never have made the deadline. We're very grateful!

About the Authors

Bill and Mardy have seven children, born between 1981 and 1995, and have homeschooled since 1986. Together they have written *Children of Character I* and *Children of Character II, from the Early Years to Adulthood.*

Bill served as a Director for the Florida Parent Home Educator Association from 1998 to 2004, and has been on the FPEA Scholarship Board from 2003 to present. He has worked for Florida Farm Bureau since 1982, now serving as a Senior PC Networking Specialist.

Jon & Sally

Bill and/or Mardy have spoken at numerous parenting, homeschool and leadership workshops in Florida (including the FPEA and HERI Conventions, and the NCFL Homeschool Fair) as well as around the country. Mardy has also written for several national publications and writes an e-mail newsletter entitled, A "Mary" Heart. Mardy currently leads a character-focused Moms' Group in Gainesville, Florida.

A Few More Resources from Bill and Mardy...

Go to www.thefreemans.org/speaking_schedule to order materials or schedule a workshop.

Children of Character I
Children of Character II, from the Early Years to Adulthood.

"A 'Mary' Heart" is a free e-mail newsletter written by Mardy to encourage moms to take time each day to sit at Jesus' feet, as Mary did in Luke 10.

Workshops/CDs:
- A Spoonful of Humor
- A Woman's Place is in the Heart
- Children of Character
- Florida Home School Law
- Getting to the Root of the Problem
- Guiding Our Teens to Maturity
- Helping Our Teens to Hear the Shepherd's Voice
- Home and School Organization Workshop Homeschooling through High School
- How to Win the Hearts of Your Husband and Children How to Do Your Best without Burning Out
- Making Altars, Cutting Ties: Identifying Ties that Bind
- Seven Keys to Winning Our Families' Hearts
- Sharpening Your Student's Skills through Political Volunteering
- Peacemaking Skills for Home and ~~Abroad~~ a Board.

- Protecting the Family
- Teaching Children How to Stand Alone
- Teaching Children to Live for a Purpose Higher than Themselves: The Role of Service in our Children's Lives
- The Differences Between False Guilt, True Guilt and True Conviction
- Traps on the Path to Character: Dealing with Pride, Fear, Guilt, Discouragement and Legalism
- Vignettes of God's Faithfulness: Stories to Encourage and Inspire
- When to Speak, When to Pray

Thank you to everyone who is praying for us, and praying for the families we try to encourage. Your prayers are felt! If the Lord brings us to mind – please take just a moment to ask Him to make His presence known wherever we are speaking, and to pour out His grace on families to receive and apply whatever truths He has for each one.
Thank you!

Footnotes

[1] *Children Learn What They Live*, Dorothy Law Nolte

[2] Pre-Scholastic Aptitude Test. Contact your local high school for testing information.

[3] Scholastic Aptitude Test (www.collegeboard.org)

[4] American College Testing Program (www.act.org)

[5] Pre-Scholastic Aptitude Test, Scholastic Aptitude Test, ACT, College Placement Test

[6] Even though some evaluators offer services on a donation basis, we ask folks to compensate them at least as much as the cost of standardized testing.

[7] Exodus 20:12

[8] This is recorded in three of the four gospels. Matthew 18:6, Mark 9:42 and Luke 17:2

[9] Matthew 10:37

[10] Matthew 6:12-15

[11] James 1:5

[12] John 10:27

[13] College Level Examination Program allows students to receive college credit through exams (www.collegeboard.org).

[14] For the rest of the story see *Children of Character II*, Chapter 4.

[15] James 4:6, 1 Peter 5:5

[16] *Better Late than Early*, Dr. Raymond Moore

[17] Matthew 19:24, Mark 10:25 and Luke 18:25

[18] 1 Samuel 2:29

[19] Matthew 6:34

[20] No pun intended.

[21] John 12:24

[22] John 15:2

[23] John 4:35

[24] 1 Timothy 3:5

[25] Romans 14:21

[26] I Corinthians 11:31

[27] Hebrews 12:6

[28] Proverbs 3:11-12

[29] Matthew 23:4

[30] Galatians 1:6-9, 2:11-14

[31] Hebrews 4:12

[32] *Spirit-Controlled Temperament*, Tim LaHaye
   The Personality Tree, Florence Littauer

[33] *The New Complete Medical and Health Encyclopedia*, first edition, 1977, page 1010

[34] *Winnie the Pooh*, A.A. Milne

[35] Bill says that the glass is neither half empty nor half full; it is simply twice as large as it needs to be.

[36] *The Birth Order Book*, Dr. Kevin Leman

[37] Dr. Donald Joy on Focus on the Family Radio Interview

[38] *Better Late Than Early*, Dr. Raymond Moore

[39] NATHHAN NEWS: NATional cHallenged Homeschoolers Associate Network, www.nathhan.com

[40] Psalm 18:25-26

[41] But encourage one another day after day, as long as it is still called "Today," so that none of you will be hardened by the deceitfulness of sin. Hebrews 3:13

[42] Matthew 12:34

[43] Job 13:15

[44] I told you I was a TV addict. See chapter 9. Bill

[45] Not because we have not power, but to make ourselves an example to you to follow us. 2 Thessalonians 3:9

[46] James 1:2

[47] Matthew 25:40

[48] Political Action Committee

[49] Special thanks to Doreen Reid for first introducing me to a nursing home ministry, and to Lena Bush for including our family in her nursing home ministry.

[50] 1 Timothy 5:8

[51] Special thanks to Sparks Giebeig for introducing our family to the ministry of feeding the hungry.

[52] Luke 11:9

[53] Matt 25:40

[54] Matt 19:30

[55] Matt 23:11

[56] Matt 26:11

[57] Rom 13:1-7

[58] *Works of Love are Works of Peace, Mother Teresa of Calcutta and the Missionaries of Charity*, a Photographic Record by Michael Collopy

[59] Psalms 27:4

[60] *The Essentials of Character,* The Macmillan Company 1915

[61] www.nheri.org

[62] College Level Examination Program

[63] 1 Corinthians 9:22

[64] *Set the Trumpet to Thy Mouth,* David Wilkerson

[65] Proverbs 6:23

[66] I Timothy 1:9-10

[67] Unless we're in a position of authority to make, enforce or judge rules over others, such as parenting young children.

[68] Someone whose standard of living doesn't match his convictions would be a hypocrite *(Do as I say, not as I do.)*
[69] Matthew 5:1-7:29
[70] John 1:14
[71] Mark 2:27
[72] Numbers 11:5,6
[73] Titus 3:5
[74] II Corinthians 10:12
[75] Luke 10:41-42
[76] 1 Timothy 4:4-5